Thank God *for* Bitcoin

Thank

The Creation,

God

Corruption, *and*

For

Redemption *of* Money

Bitcoin

ROBERT BREEDLOVE · J.M. BUSH · GABE HIGGINS · LYLE PRATT
GEORGE MEKHAIL · JIMMY SONG · JULIA TOURIANSKI · DEREK WALTCHACK

Published by TGFB Media
www.tgfb.com

Bitcoin and Bible Group, *Thank God For Bitcoin:
The Creation, Corruption, and Redemption of Money*

Copyright © 2020, 2026 by Bitcoin and Bible Group.
First edition published 2020 by Bitcoin and Bible Group.
Second edition published 2026 by TGFB Media.

Book design by Robert J. Hewitt III, Livingstones Studio
Printed in the United States of America.

All rights reserved. No part of this publication may be reproduced, stored in a retrieval system, or transmitted in any form by any means, electronic, mechanical, photocopy, recording, or otherwise, without prior permission of the author, except as provided by USA copyright law.

Unless otherwise noted, all Scripture quotations are from the ESV® Bible (The Holy Bible, English Standard Version®), copyright © 2001 by Crossway, a publishing ministry of Good News Publishers. Used by permission.

Paperback ISBN: 979-8-9923493-5-1
Hardcover ISBN: 979-8-9923493-4-4
ePub ISBN: 979-8-9923493-6-8

Library of Congress Cataloging-in-Publication Data is on file with the publisher.

*For the glory of God
and the good of people everywhere.*

Contents

Foreword to the Second Edition		IX
Preface		XIII
1	Understanding Money	1
2	The History of Money	13
3	Inflation	27
4	The Problems with Fiat Money	41
5	Money and Politics	49
6	The Moral Consequences of Corrupt Money	65
7	How Bad Money Corrupts the Church	79
8	Bitcoin, a More Moral Money	91
9	The Redemption of Money	105
Afterword		123

Foreword to the Second Edition

IN 2013, we had a ransomware attack on a laptop at work, and the demands were clear: we had to send them $500 worth of Bitcoin for the password to unlock our laptop. We sent them about five Bitcoins, and a few minutes later we had our laptop back. Unfortunately, we did not buy any extra.

The next time I bought Bitcoin would be January 30th, 2021, which is when I really started my journey. Robinhood had just halted trading on the GameStop stock, and even though I wasn't in a GME trade, I recognized the danger. That was the catalyst I needed to buy Bitcoin and that led me down a rabbit hole to eventually read the Bitcoin whitepaper and become a Bitcoiner.

Our money is broken. Today many Americans realize this fact, but many can't explain what's wrong and search for answers in the wrong places, or more likely just assume it is their lot in life and give up. I chuckle at that thought because I was introduced to Bitcoin through theft in 2013, but I know now that Bitcoin is the answer to the broken system. Exodus 20:15 commands, "You shall not steal," but the theft of our work is built into the world's monetary system. We are on a constant consumer hamster wheel because the Federal Reserve's 2% inflation target has mandated debasement by law. By decree, or fiat, our money has become an abomination. Most people don't understand the compounding effects of time and money. Once you start researching Bitcoin, you start to understand.

As Christians, we are citizens of a different realm, but as ambassadors for a short time here on earth, we must be wise with the gifts that God has given us to steward. In the Parable of the Talents, Jesus told of the wicked servant who didn't even put the money in the bank to earn interest. That servant was condemned not for losing money but for being lazy. He failed to use his skills with what had been entrusted to him. The master expected at minimum that the servant would have put the capital to work at a bank.

Today, our banks rarely give interest above the inflation rate. In fact, for much of recent history, real interest rates have been negative. This means that the "safe" option of putting money in the bank, guarantees the slow confiscation of your wealth. The parable assumes a monetary system where preservation of value is possible. Our current system makes faithful stewardship nearly impossible for the average person.

I have come to the conclusion that Christians must find a way to jettison fiat dollars and build on sound money. Christ taught that the wise man builds his house upon the rock, while the foolish man builds on sand. Fiat currency is shifting sand. The purchasing power of the dollar has fallen more than 97% since the Federal Reserve's creation. From the 1970s until today, the destruction has accelerated. Bitcoin is a rock—fixed in supply, immutable in its rules, resistant to manipulation.

In the book of Joel, God warns of the destruction that comes when the locust, the cankerworm, and the caterpillar devour the land. Inflation is the modern cankerworm, slowly and steadily eating away at everything we've worked to build. Bitcoin provides a storehouse that the worm cannot touch. Since the fourth quarter of 2021, I have been dollar-cost averaging between 1% and 5% of profits from our business, Classical Conversations, into Bitcoin. Our treasury is not as big as I would like, but we now have some protection from what the worm will eat.

This book you're about to read makes a case that needs to be heard in every church, every Christian home, and every believer's heart. The intersection of faith and finance is not peripheral to the gospel—it's part of how we live out our faith in a fallen world. When we choose sound money over debasing currency, we're choosing justice over theft, truth over manipulation, and stewardship over passivity.

Thank God for Bitcoin. And thank God for the authors who have taken the time to show us why Bitcoin matters not just economically, but theologically and morally. The path forward requires both understanding and action. May this book provide the former and inspire the latter.

ROBERT BORTINS
CEO Classical Conversations
November 2025

Preface

MONEY IS DEEPLY SPIRITUAL.

After all, relationships are spiritual and money is a big part of relationships. Business relationships are defined by money. Family and personal relationships are often influenced by money. Money even relates strangers to each other through trade.

Few relationships have no component of money because money plays a significant role in how we fit into society. 1 Timothy 6:10 says, "For the love of money is a root of all sorts of evil." Love of money is the motive for all kinds of sin: murder, theft, deceit, and resentment. Money is used to enslave, which we call usury. By contrast, money is also a force for good. It enables charity, kindness, and expressions of love. It empowers, motivates, and rewards the creation of beneficial things. Money is the tool by which we can store up the fruits of our labor for rainier days. Money is vital, and present in almost everything we do.

Despite the spiritual significance of money, many Christians treat it as banal, lowbrow, worldly, or worse. This attitude is not consistent with what is taught in the Bible, which highlights the importance of having a righteous and wise approach to money.

The Bible is full of monetary metaphors. Even the story of salvation that is woven throughout the entirety of Scripture is described in the language of money: payment, debt, forgiveness, redemption.

Because money is deeply relational, the spiritual repercussions of money are broad. Greed, envy, and lust for power are just some of the many negative consequences of its worship. While these sins are rightly condemned, little is discussed about the system that aggravates them.

This book is about the monetary system that we live in and its moral and spiritual implications. The monetary system is to money what the food production system is to food. There is much going on behind the scenes that affects the final product. This isn't a book about personal finances and money management. What we're going to describe in these pages are the moral and spiritual implications of this process. In other words, we're going to focus on how the sausage gets made.

The goal of this book is to unpack the basics about what money is, examine the troubling realities of our modern monetary system, and propose a morally sound and hopeful alternative to the economic water we all swim in each day. The pervasive influence of money is consequential to who we are collectively, and the fruit of our monetary system is a reflection of our values. With that in mind, here's how the book is organized.

Chapters 1 and 2 answer the question: *What is money?* Chapter 1 describes money from a theological perspective. Specifically, we cover money's role in our lives and, consequently, the spiritual situation we find ourselves in. Chapter 2 describes money from a historical perspective. This chapter goes through the many innovations and subsequent moral failings of money, starting with metal bullion to the modern-day debt-based fiat system.

Chapters 3 and 4 describe the tools by which our modern monetary system has corrupted the rest of society. Chapter 3 analyzes inflation. We cover inflation and how it has destroyed many countries. Chapter 4 analyzes fiat money. We explain how fiat money works and how it is used as a tool for theft.

Chapters 5, 6, and 7 examine the moral consequences of the current system. Chapter 5 looks at how our monetary system has corrupted political systems. Chapter 6 focuses on the individual consequences while Chapter 7 focuses on the Church at large.

Chapters 8 and 9 explore what we can do about these problems. Chapter 8 proposes Bitcoin as a morally superior alternative. Chapter 9 concludes the book with ways that Bitcoin redeems money politically, individually, and spiritually.

The spiritual realm is where we find meaning. Our time, relationships, and beliefs are unseen yet ever present in our experience. The state of the world is the sum total of our relationships, and relationships are greatly shaped by our monetary system. By understanding the monetary system, we can work toward a better world.

This change, however, must start with ourselves. The Bible calls this wisdom, something that's better than money:

> *"How much better to get wisdom than gold, to get insight rather than silver!"*
> — *Proverbs 16:16*

There is much insight and wisdom we hope to convey about money in the following pages. Let us begin, then, with this basic question: "What is Money?"

Chapter 1: Understanding Money

> "My people perish for lack of knowledge."
> — Hosea 4:6

MONEY.

What comes to mind when you hear that word? How does it make you feel? Ambitious? Overwhelmed? Pressured? Why do you think it makes you feel that way?

Your answers reveal the power that money has over you. And you are not the only one. For millions of people all over the world, money has brought on feelings of anxiety, joy, heartbreak, stress, and humility. Money has triggered suicide and it has elevated entire countries out of poverty. It has destroyed marriages, and it has allowed large families to thrive for generations. Great wars have been financed with and fought over money. The effects of money are an integral part of the human experience. In our day and age, those effects are inescapable no matter your lifestyle choices or your personal view of the current monetary system.

The New Testament is filled with terms and analogies that come from money, yet the subject is too often taboo among Christians. If talked about at all, it is often a sermon on the importance of tithing or a Bible study about financial stewardship. But these topics are all about *using* money and not about *understanding* money itself.

We tend to focus on what we can purchase with money or where we can make more money or how we can spend less money. We may have learned from economics that money is a store of value, a medium of exchange, and a unit of account. We acknowledge money as a fact of life, but we rarely think to question our basic assumptions about money.

— Perhaps you have never asked yourself these questions:
— What is money?
— Why does it exist?
— What is it designed to do?
— How does it work?

Few people today have a clear understanding of how money originates, its many types, or the various ways it influences social morality.

Why?

Wouldn't it make sense to prioritize education about something so fundamental to human relationships? Charles Munger, Vice Chairman of Berkshire Hathaway, once said, "Show me the incentive and I'll show you the outcome." The reason for the lack of basic understanding of the nature of money is simple: there are massive incentives in keeping money obscure, complex, and seemingly impossible to understand.

The prophet Hosea, speaking on behalf of God, rebuked the rulers of Israel for failing to rightly lead and teach His people. God explains that where basic understanding lacks in a society, oppression, injustice and suffering won't be far behind. The powerful few use the lack of knowledge to exploit the many. The general lack of knowledge about money today is a symptom of the exploitation taking place, hidden behind the obscurity set in place by those in power. The goal of this book is to shine a light into that darkness. This book seeks to explain what money is, how it is often corrupted, and what can be done to fix the problems that exist.

The Role of Money

> "For where your treasure is, there your heart will be also."
> — Matthew 6:21

Money enables us to take what we have and trade it for what we need.

Money is a source of power. It can help overcome limitations in life. No wonder many respect it, love it, live for it, and do whatever it takes to obtain it.

The way we use money demonstrates what we believe to be real, good, right, and important. When we spend money on something, we are in effect stating, "I need this and it is useful to me." The way we spend money reveals what we love and what we fear. Money, in other words, expresses the values of the spender.

Our modern American society values money the same way that most human societies treat their gods. We tend to view it as an unquestioned good, sowing peace, security, freedom, and joy wherever it is found.

Like most gods, money is a god that requires sacrifice. And these sacrifices are made in the form of work. Families, time, and sleep are also sacrificed in the quest to attain money. Working to acquire money is not inherently wrong or immoral, but we need to be aware of the danger of viewing monetary gain as the ultimate prize.

It is helpful to consider some often-overlooked factors.

First, the kind of work a person does matters. Hitmen can make lots of money, but the fact that we *can* do something lucratively doesn't mean we *should*.

Second, our motivation for making money matters. Money can't guarantee safety, longevity, or happiness. Many wealthy people get sick, are killed, or tragically take their own lives. Many of the most miserable people in the world are obscenely rich. Money can buy houses, private jets, and even sports teams, but it can't buy joy. Money, as a means for ultimate fulfillment, over-promises and under-delivers. On the contrary, the apostle Paul told Timothy that "godliness with contentment is great gain." Money can solve many physical problems that we face, but it was made as a tool to help us love God and love others, not as a place to search for self-worth, identity, and happiness.

Third, the type of money that we use has tremendous consequences on those who use it. All money is not created equal. Money is a tool, and tools are designed and made only after a need or objective has already been identified. If a tool is designed badly, or the goals and objectives of a tool are toward immoral ends, then those who use it will be affected.

This third factor is what we will investigate in this book. Understanding what money was intended to be and how it became corrupted will shine light on the problems that exist.

What is it about money that strikes fear and awkwardness into communities, and particularly the Christian community? How can we, as believers, navigate the challenges of money or appreciate its potential for benevolence if we don't understand what money is?

Money, at its most fundamental level, is a gift from God.

Created in the Image of God

> *"God created man in His own image, in the image of God He created him;"* — Genesis 1:27

One of the advantages of being made in the image of God is that we have the divinely-delegated authority to create useful things with our hands. Having this ability means we can turn chaos into order, which is an enormous responsibility. As G.K. Chesterton said, *"A dead thing can go with the stream, but only a living thing can go against it."*

We express this principle—the bearing of God's image—primarily through our daily work and in voluntary exchanges. By trading with one another, a community can collectively work to produce more output than individuals could in isolation. By collaborating, we can create more through a shared sense of purpose, belonging, and community. This is what we call the *anti-entropic principle*.

Money is the most easily tradable asset in any society. It is a primary tool for collaborative human action—a medium of exchange that has the potential to expand and deepen the nature of our work. A tool this critical to the flourishing of civilization is clearly a gift from God. However, the ancient temptation of desiring more than our daily bread and lusting for riches has presented us with a dilemma about the object of our worship.

Worship of Money

> "No one can serve two masters. Either you will hate the one and love the other, or you will be devoted to the one and despise the other. You cannot serve both God and money." — Matthew 6:24

We consistently face the temptation of worshiping the creation rather than the Creator. We are seduced into focusing more on the gifts than the Giver. But as Jesus said, this is an unsustainable conflict. We will take the form of a servant, either loving God or loving money.

Although money is poorly understood and rarely discussed at a deep level, our devotion to it is often open and unabashed. This devotion goes beyond pop-culture wealth signaling or keeping up with our neighbors. We associate money with freedom, happiness, and self-worth. How much money we have directly impacts not only the way others see us, but often how we see ourselves.

Our obsession with money doesn't discriminate between classes. Rich, poor, or middle class, many of us seem to have the same obsession: how best to earn, save, spend, and invest our money. Are we just naturally greedy? Why do so many people put economic gain above the well-being of others or even themselves? The truth is that self-interest is hardwired into our worldly existence. We can only hope to create systems that do not turn self-interest into greed.

Truly understanding what money is will reduce the power that money has over us. Money is corrupted and aggravates unsavory temptations, robbing us of our freedom. Sadly, not much is taught in churches about what money is or how money functions. Many church leaders are dealing with the same negative influences and misunderstandings about money, so it is not surprising they don't preach about it.

Money does not have to rule our lives. It doesn't have to be an obsession, and it doesn't have to be a source of pain in the world. Money can be received with thanksgiving and viewed as a good gift that serves us, not the other way around. Understand that all money is not created equal. Both moral and immoral money have existed throughout history. Once we understand the negative changes to our money, we can avoid the immoral incentives inherent to the unsound money that we have today. But before we can understand how today's money has failed us, we must take a step back and understand what *work* is and its relationship to money.

The Law of Sowing and Reaping

> "Do not be deceived, God is not mocked; for whatever a man sows, this he will also reap." — Galatians 6:7

God could have made any kind of world. God could have made a world where we only need to think of something and immediately receive it. God could have instituted a world where prayer is the basis for accomplishing everything in the world and every request made to Him is granted.

God could have served as humanity's butler, directly creating everything that would ever be made.

"Hungry?" – poof – "Here's a sandwich."

"Thirsty?" – poof – "Here's some lemonade."

Instead, we find a God who desires to share this inspired responsibility with all of creation. While God did miraculously create things in the beginning, He designed us to be co-laborers in the world and gave us autonomy. Successive creation involves natural perpetuation.

That is, God gives living things the will and ability to sustain and multiply themselves. The soil where the seed is to be planted needs to be dug and softened in order to provide the seed with the best chance of producing fruit. Without this *sowing* there can be no *reaping*. Without *planting*, there can be no *harvest*. Growth must be preceded by work.

As Paul states in his letter to the Galatians, the relationship between work and reward is fixed and immutable. Sowing and reaping is an ingrained principle in our world. Investment and its returns are a part of God's design, making work an integral part of being human.

Work Versus Theft

> *"He who steals must steal no longer but rather he must labor, performing with his own hands what is good so that he will have something to share with one who has need."* — Ephesians 4:28

We cannot understand money without understanding work. Money is an integral part of life *because* work is an integral part of life. Work is what we do in order to create something of value for ourselves and others. Theft is the opposite; it is taking something of value from others.

Economists would say that stealing is zero-sum, that is, there is no net benefit to the collective. The thief wins only at the expense of others. In other words, work is creative while theft is destructive.

The eighth commandment says that stealing is wrong. Even the secular world knows that theft is against Natural Law because stealing offends us on a primal level. To steal is to dissolve the interpersonal trust necessary for fruitful cooperation. The emotions that go along with the injustice of theft are inborn and can even be observed in very young children. Similar sentiments have been noted amongst primates and other mammals. Even the most ardent Communist, who may claim to not believe in private property or to hate money, will be distraught if another person robs him.

Work is hard. It makes something out of nothing—the proverbial "fruits of labor." Work adds value, benefiting people, communities, and countries by creating new goods and services that improve people's lives. Work that adds value should get rewarded. Theft should be punished because it destroys value. Theft does damage to the glory of God's image that we bear and is therefore dehumanizing and immoral.

Where Money Fits In

> *"Do to others as you would have them do to you."*
> — Luke 6:31

Jesus said that we could sum up God's design for humanity in two commandments: love God, and love our neighbor. God's heart for humanity from the beginning was to create a world where we would voluntarily love one another.

Most people live in communities because humans are interdependent and need to cooperate to thrive. Having a community allows individuals to develop specialized skills and trade the fruits of their labor. This can be centrally-controlled by a governing body or voluntarily entered into based on demand. We'll discuss centrally controlled "cooperation" in Chapter 5, but the main way that communities functioned throughout history has been through voluntary exchange.

This is where money comes in.

Money acts as a powerful tool to measure the value of work. One of the main benefits of communities is the ability to specialize. It would be very hard for any modern person to have to grow their own food, build their own house, and make their own clothes. Specialization means that each person produces different goods and services. How valuable is growing a crop of wheat? Or building a house? Or making a shirt? Money gives us a tool to exchange and measure all of these things.

A sound money system also allows us to save. We can sacrifice our time today for money that can be redeemed for something of similar value tomorrow. Money allows us to save for the future, working more during good times to save our earnings for the bad times to come. When an entire community does this, money helps create security and safety for its people.

Money's Design

> *"Do not store up for yourselves treasures on earth, where moths and vermin destroy, and where thieves break in and steal. But store up for yourselves treasures in heaven, where moths and vermin do not destroy, and where thieves do not break in and steal."*
> — Matthew 6:19-20

We can think of money as promises or favors that can be traded. The "rich" are those who are owed a lot of favors for their work, and the "poor" are those who are owed few. Money is a way to keep track of the value that has been provided to someone in the community at some point in the past. Those who provide more value at one point in time can be justly rewarded later.

If this accounting system of favors sounds familiar, it is because this is exactly how Jesus describes our storing up of treasures in heaven. We may not be rewarded for serving the poor and oppressed in this life, but God assures us our reward in the next life.

Money is integral to the design of civilization. To be clear, even the godliest monetary systems are a shadow of the real thing, but the true purpose of money reveals God's intention. In a moral monetary system, money is earned through voluntary work. In an immoral monetary system, money is taken involuntarily.

Theft = Stealing Work

> *"The thief comes only to steal and kill and destroy; I came that they may have life, and have it abundantly."* — John 10:10

Theft corrupts justice by allowing those that have not contributed to the community to reap its fruits. Work is earning just rewards, or value exchanged for value. Theft is an unjust seizure of value and, by nature, unearned.

Profitable work requires evaluating the community to figure out what it needs, and then filling that need by creating a quality product or service.

Failure to do so will result in work that doesn't provide value, meaning less or no money will be earned.

If a farmer decides to produce potatoes in a town where there are already hundreds of potato farmers, his crop may not even sell. If a farmer decides to produce the most delicious potatoes in the same town, he will probably sell more than anyone else.

Prosperous people in a moral and free market attain their position by serving the community. The money they earn as a result of this service is an indirect measure of the trust placed in them by the community. In a free market, it is the servants of society who benefit the most. The emotion, time, and virtue needed for valuable work is part of what makes the work valuable.

Theft, on the other hand, requires a lot less time, investment, virtue, and work. Theft only provides value to the thieves and is always at the cost of the community. Today, theft has become deeply integrated into our monetary system.

As we will explore and explain more deeply in these pages, every dollar printed is property stolen from the community. This thieving, rotten core of the current financial system is antithetical to the original purpose of money.

One name for the Devil is "the thief who kills and steals and destroys." We imitate God when we work, and we imitate the Devil when we steal.

Conclusion

Many will maintain that money is morally neutral—that it is just a tool and it all depends on who uses it and how. Using money to hire a hitman, for example, would be evil, but using money to feed the hungry would be good. Yet this says nothing about the moral characteristics of money; it only describes what someone did with it.

Money is a unique tool. Since it is a special good used for trade, the nature of its construction holds a heavy influence on social morality. The moral neutrality of money assumes that all forms of money are the same. The truth is, there is moral and immoral money, and the type of money we use can and does influence our actions.

In the next chapter, we will discuss how money comes in many forms, including commodity money, credit money, and fiat money. Each presents different economic incentives and temptations. The form of money we use matters because certain forms of money tempt us towards theft more than others.

When money is hard to steal, the community that uses it tends to have a system that rewards people for providing value through work. When money is easy to steal, it incentivizes theft, which discourages people from providing value through work and directly hurts the community.

The ideal money would make honest work easy and theft difficult. By contrast, morally repugnant money would make honest work difficult and theft easy. Unfortunately, this is the case of the monetary system we have today.

Next, we will explore the history of money to see how we got to where we are today. We'll look at how each change has made trade easier, as well as how it introduced new temptations for theft.

Chapter 2: The History of Money

> "Enter through the narrow gate; for the gate is wide and the way is broad that leads to destruction, and there are many who enter through it. For the gate is small and the way is narrow that leads to life, and there are few who find it." — Matthew 7:13-14

MONETARY HISTORY is rife with misguided intentions, temptations, and unintended consequences. Different civilizations have utilized different monies, which has shaped not only their economies, but their day-to-day life, legal systems, and governments.

Money has also gradually become easier and more convenient to use for transacting. As we explore the history of money, we'll focus on why certain changes were made and the moral consequences of those changes. Money has had a variety of moral impacts throughout history.

In a sense, humanity's struggle with money is similar to the search for what Jesus described as "the narrow gate" in the book of Matthew. The paper currency we use in modern days is comparable to the wide and broad gate of convenience and laziness. This has led to abuses and corruption through the control of money. War, slavery, and famine are just some of the consequences.

Before we go further in unpacking this thought, let's revisit the role of money.

The Role of Money

Money is a tool for trade. It is quite simply the most tradable asset in any society. Money helps move value across time and space. Of course, given that very generic definition, nearly any physical object can serve in that role. Historically, anything from seashells to silver has been used as money. Even today, mackerel cans and 150-oz Tide detergent bottles are used as money in prisons and inner cities, respectively. These are seemingly odd choices, but they provide clues about the role of money in society.

Let's look at an example of two people who want to engage in trade; one person grows oranges and the other owns a house. Perhaps the orange grower wants a house, and the house owner wants oranges. This situation cannot be simply resolved through trade for a few reasons.

The first problem is one of scale. It is unlikely that the house owner would want the number of oranges that would be equivalent to the value of a house, and trading fractions of a house is not practical.

The second problem is that of location. The orange grower wants a house, but the available house may not be in the right area. Houses cannot easily be moved from one place to another, though oranges can be.

The third problem concerns time. Even if the house owner wants a lot of oranges and the house happens to be in the right location, there is still the problem of producing enough oranges to buy a house. To grow the number of oranges required to trade for a house may take years, by which time the earlier crops of oranges will have spoiled. The house is better in this regard as it's more durable.

This is why society needs money. Money acts as the medium of exchange to solve the problems of trading across various scales, locations, and times. So, what are the properties that enable money to solve such problems?

Properties of Money

First, money should be **divisible**. It must have the capacity to be subdivided into small amounts so that scale isn't a problem. One must have the ability to use money to pay for both oranges and houses.

Second, money should be **portable**, or able to be easily transported from one place to another. That is, money should solve the problem of location.

Third, money should be **durable**, or be resistant to physical degradation over time. This is why, in the above example, oranges would not serve as an ideal money.

Fourth, money should be **recognizable**, or easy to verify its authenticity. It should not be something that can be easily faked.

Finally, money should be **scarce**, so that its supply is resistant to manipulation over time. Money should hold its value and be able to pay for goods not just now but also into the future. Scarcity may be the most important property of money, as it provides a check on counterfeiting, supply manipulation, and theft.

These five properties—divisibility, portability, durability, recognizability, and scarcity—are why a certain asset emerges as the preferred money in a society. Finding a good that exhibits all five properties is difficult. A good that deeply satisfies all five properties of money is akin to the "narrow gate."

Standardized Weights

> "A false balance is an abomination to the Lord, but a just weight is his delight." — Proverbs 11:1

The ability for a good to preserve value over time is not common. This is because if something has value, people will try to make or find more of it. For example, a cell phone in the '80s was very expensive and considered a luxury. Today, cell phones are much cheaper and owned by 70% of adults around the world. This is why we don't store cell phones as our savings.

A good that can be easily produced in large quantities offers a poor basis for money. But something that's difficult to produce in quantity can work as an effective form of money. Gold is the classic example. Gold is not easy to produce in large quantities. Many people have tried and mostly failed, despite several technological innovations. Gold is scarce and not only hard to find but also expensive to extract from the earth.

These qualities of scarcity and durability allow gold to preserve value over time. Economists would say that gold is hard to inflate or that gold is a "hard" money, as in hard-to-produce. A good that inflates is something that can easily be produced in large quantities. We will discuss the concept of inflation more thoroughly in the next chapter. Economists call money based on a good that's easy to produce "easy" or "soft" money. Easy money doesn't preserve value very well.

Precious metals mostly satisfy several of the vital properties of money: divisibility, durability, recognizability, and scarcity. Of these metals, gold exhibited the greatest scarcity, and therefore became the most valuable. The amount of gold produced in a given year was predictably small. People then trusted that gold's value would be preserved over time. However, since gold was exceptionally rare and heavy, it suffered in terms of divisibility and portability, which gave silver better utility as a transactional money.

Other goods that have acted as money in eras past—such as glass beads, seashells, and even rai stones—were once hard to produce. Eventually, however, all these ancient monies failed because new technologies were used to produce them in large quantities. As we will see, excessive supply production (a.k.a. inflation) always destroys the utility of money by compromising its scarcity.

Back to the portability of money, weighing metal in ancient times made trade extremely cumbersome. Shekel means "weight" in Hebrew, and one shekel corresponds to about half an ounce. There was a standard sanctuary shekel to measure all other weights. Most words for money around the world—including pound, peso, and lira—are measures of weight because money was nearly always a metal denominated by weight.

This did not make for the most straightforward exchanges. Imagine, for example, having to weigh your money at the market every time you wanted to buy something. This not only made trade slow and inconvenient, but it also led to dishonest merchants using misleading weights in order to steal from their customers. This practice became widespread to the point where the above verse in Proverbs condemns it directly.

Additionally, the problem of counterfeiting was ever present. There was no fancy marker that a merchant could use to verify the authenticity of the money a customer was trying to use to pay for goods. It wasn't easy to confirm that something was really pure gold or pure silver. Unscrupulous people would mix these metals with cheaper metals to get more weight for less cost. This is an early form of counterfeiting, which has sadly plagued money for its entire history.

Coins

> *"Or what woman, if she has ten silver coins and loses one coin, does not light a lamp and sweep the house and search carefully until she finds it?"* — Luke 15:8

Gold and silver in their original, raw, bullion form were somewhat easy to counterfeit and inconvenient to trade. This created a need in the market for a more reliable standard, which led to the next monetary innovation: minted coinage. To "mint" a coin means to mark it with a symbol that would be widely recognized and much more difficult to counterfeit. The Kings of Lydia were among the first coinage innovators, minting gold and silver coins around 700 BC[1].

By minting coins, the Lydian Kings were able to eliminate the need for weighing bullion in each transaction, which increased trade. They were able to grow very rich by issuing standardized coins of different denominations; Lydian kings such as King Midas, King Croesus, and King Gyges[2] are famous to this day for their fabulous wealth. King Midas is known in mythology as the one with the golden touch, a story about the all-consuming effects of greed. King Croesus financed one of the seven wonders of the world—the Temple of Artemis—which Paul would encounter in Ephesus during his ministry. King Gyges was able to subjugate a large territory by gifting the Oracle at

---

1. Source: Heather Whipps, The Profound History of Coins, Live Science
2. Source: Lydians, King Croesus and the World's First Money, Facts and Details

Delphi talents of gold. These kings became legendary all because of a simple monetary innovation—coins.

The usage of coins from then on became the standard. Keep in mind that coins were pretty much unknown in the Old Testament. Roughly seven hundred years later, their use had grown so common that Jesus gave the parable of the lost coin in Luke.

Coins made theft harder. No longer could people use dishonest weights to cheat others, as the coins had a standard weight. However, coinage didn't prevent theft completely.

Coin clipping was a widespread practice, in which owners would shave the coins slightly so as to not make it noticeable, then pass them off as the full standard weight. The practice, unfortunately, mars most coins that survive from that era, giving us insight into how widespread this new type of theft was. There were even variations on clipping such as sweating, which was putting a bunch of coins in a bag and shaking them until tiny pieces of the coin broke off, which could then be melted.

These examples of theft were conducted by individuals, but far more theft was conducted by the minters themselves through the process of debasement. *Debasement* is the practice of melting the coins and adding a less expensive metal to mix, or alloy, with them. By debasing coins, a minter can create more coins for the same amount of metal. Thus, debasement is a form of counterfeiting.

Coins that underwent debasement during their minting looked very similar, so only a trained person could tell the difference. The progression of debasement can be clearly seen with the example of the denarius. A denarius during Jesus's time had 3.9g of silver in it. Two hundred years later, a denarius had 1.7g of silver. A mere 50 years after that, the only silver left in Roman coins was a negligible amount in the coating.

The denarius was introduced in 211 BC[3] with 4.5g of silver. Augustus debased the denarius to 3.9g of silver and Nero debased the denarius to 3.4g of silver. This allowed them to raise revenues without upsetting their populace by raising taxes, but there were unintended consequences. Prices inevitably rose following increases in the money supply. An expanding money supply

---

3. Source: The Fall of the Roman denarius, Money Museum

always leads directly to price inflation; a devalued currency means more units are necessary to buy things.

Predictably, these Roman Emperors did not announce this debasement, and it took time for the community to figure this out. In the meantime, the Roman government spent their coins for goods and services before the increase in prices, thereby redistributing wealth from citizens to the state. Over time, debasement became commonplace to the point that, by the reign of Claudius II in 268 AD, Roman-minted coins were almost entirely made of bronze, not silver. This led to economic turmoil throughout the Roman Empire and eventually contributed to its collapse.

Nearly every sovereign nation claimed the right to mint coins and many of them, like the Bourbon dynasty in France and the Han dynasty in China, ended up debasing the coins and stealing from their people. Why was this the case? Governments generally want to spend more money than they have, and additional expenditures require additional revenue. Taxation is the primary form of government revenue, but citizens tend to resist explicit taxation.

Stealing from the populace through debasement, however, is a more subtle and deceptive means of taxation. Debasement gives governments a sneaky way to get revenue without paying the public relations price associated with explicit taxes. In other words, currency debasement is stealth taxation, and in case you were wondering, it is still being practiced today.

The Emergence of Gold

> "Now Abram was very rich in livestock, in silver and in gold."
> — Genesis 13:2

When most people think of gold, they think of wealth, gaudiness, and maybe dragon hoards or peg legged pirates. This association between gold and wealth is almost intuitive. But why do we associate wealth with gold? Why has gold been sought after and used as money for so long? What characteristics does gold have that make it good money?

First, gold is rare. Hence, it is called a *precious* metal. Gold had to be mined, a process that required land, labor, and specialized equipment. In other words, gold has been and continues to be difficult to produce, which makes gold scarce over long periods of time.

Second, gold is a reliably stable element and will not deteriorate or corrode over time, unlike most metals. For example, the aerospace industry uses gold for critical parts where corrosion could be fatal. This also means almost every ounce of gold ever mined is still part of the existing supply.

Third, gold is interchangeable and malleable. About 60% of gold's global supply is held in the form of jewelry. Gold can be formed, measured, transferred, and easily stored without spoilage.

The free market tends to preserve value in whatever is hardest to produce. This is because newly produced units dilute the value of existing units. Since gold is more difficult to produce than every other form of physical money, gold emerged in the late 19th century as the monetary standard around the world.

Network Effects of Money

The other reason that gold emerged in the late 19th century as the standard form of money is due to what we call *network effects*. Network effects are the benefits a product or service gains as more people use it. For example, eBay is more useful for buyers when there are more people selling, and more useful for sellers when there are more buyers. Networks are more useful when more people participate because it makes more connections possible.

Network effects create a strong winner-take-all environment, which leads to a single dominant platform instead of many smaller ones. This winner-take-all condition of network effects works similarly for money, driving users to adopt a single monetary standard. For money, each new network participant makes the entire network more valuable, because more trade is possible.

Expressing prices in single money also simplifies trade. The late 19th-century era is often referred to as the "Gilded Age" in part due to the emerging gold standard. The network effects of money caused country after country to adopt the gold standard, which in turn made international trade easier and more convenient.

Banknotes

> *Jesus replied and said, "A man was going down from Jerusalem to Jericho, and fell among robbers, and they stripped him and beat him, and went away leaving him half dead."* — Luke 10:30

Back when money was primarily coins, there was a problem: any time trade occurred, the coins had to be transported. This was fine for small transactions, as the payer only had to bring a small number of coins, but large transactions were literally hard to carry out.

First, transporting large quantities of coins is physically difficult. Even now, five million dollars in hundred-dollar bills would weigh over 100 pounds. Transporting a large amount of low-value coins such as copper was challenging to say the least.

Second, it opened up the payer to the possibility of significant loss. Transportation could cause accidental loss—as sunken treasure ships of yesteryear will testify. Transportation also risked robbery as in the parable of the Good Samaritan mentioned in the scripture above.

Third, due to the previous two challenges, transporting large amounts of coins was expensive. To secure the coins, it was common for the owners to pay armed guards to transport coinage long distances. Even then, owners risked the continuous threat of betrayal, incompetence, and accidents.

At this point, two innovations were introduced: banks and banknotes. The earliest banks, which were located in Venice, provided a warehousing service for money, allowing the depositors to not have to worry about securing money themselves. As more people kept their money at banks, the act of withdrawing money, then paying and depositing the money again, could be made much more efficient using a representation of the money in the bank vault, instead of the money itself.

That representation was the *banknote*. The holder of the banknote could redeem the banknote for money at any time, but the banknote wasn't itself money. For all practical purposes, though, banknotes acted like gold, silver, or copper in the bank vault, and were much more convenient to use. Carrying banknotes to the next town was safer, easier, and less costly than carrying metal.

Ultimately, banknotes allowed even more trade, especially over larger distances. Unfortunately, banknotes also made it incredibly easy for banks to steal from their depositors. Banks began lending out the money stored in their vaults. This meant that the borrower and the depositor assumed there was a corresponding amount of precious metal backing each banknote. In reality, the quantity of banknotes was significantly higher than the metal they represented.

This act of lending out money without specific money to back it up is what we call *fractional-reserve banking*. Fractional-reserve banking is a more sophisticated form of the ancient fraud of counterfeiting. Venetian banks were first created in 1157. Less than a century later, in 1255, there were already bank failures due to fractional-reserve banking.

Central Banks

> *"Do not store up for yourselves treasures on earth, where moth and rust destroy, and where thieves break in and steal."* — Matthew 6:19

Under fractional-reserve banking, if a large number of people wanted to redeem their banknotes all at the same time, the bank would not have enough money to pay them, leading to a situation we call *bankruptcy*. Fractional reserve banks lend money that does not exist—an inherently fraudulent act.

You might ask, "But isn't it good to give people loans?" The honest way to lend would be to get depositors to agree not to withdraw for a period of time that matches the term of the loan.

Sadly, most banks throughout history haven't done the honest thing and most have had trouble with insolvency. This is the issue one faces with giving trust to a third party. The temptation to steal is ever present.

When paper currency is backed with gold, this is called a *gold standard*. In the early 20th century, most of the world's monetary system functioned this way. As banknotes were so much more convenient than gold coins, gold gathered in bank vaults. Transfers between banks started to become as risky and inconvenient as using gold coins, so there emerged the innovation of central banks.

A *central bank* is a bank for a bunch of other banks. Instead of the costly process of banks sending each other gold whenever a customer from one bank deposited a check from a customer of another bank, a central bank allows the banks to keep much of their collective gold in one place and use a ledger to settle the difference.

Approximately one hundred years ago, banks still needed to hold some gold, since customers would occasionally redeem their banknotes for gold. The bulk of the bank money, however, could be put into a central repository so banks could settle with one another instead of making costly trips back and forth.

The temptations of central banks are many. Central banks make it very easy for the government to steal the money because it's all in one place. The theft is almost always in the form of a loan to the government at artificially low interest rates. The government takes the gold from the central bank in exchange for a bunch of IOUs. Historically, such theft is often done to fund wars.

This naturally leads to the government suspending the convertibility of banknotes. Suspended convertibility means that the banknotes can no longer be exchanged for their worth in gold. When the government steals the money in this form, the central bank is now insolvent, meaning the bank no longer has enough gold to cover all their depositors. However, suspending convertibility prevents the central bank from going bankrupt.

From a moral perspective, suspending convertibility is breaking a contractual promise, and is a form of lying. Banknotes are supposed to be representations of the underlying money. By suspending convertibility, banks break promises made to the depositors. The truth is, this has been the system by which banks have operated for so long that we have grown completely accustomed to it. No one would expect to receive their savings from a bank in the form of gold pieces.

In any other business, such practices would be considered a scam or an outright fraud. Imagine, for example, if leaving a car at a carwash possibly meant that you wouldn't get your car back for two months, or at all! Until the advent of modern laws protecting banks, banks that suspended convertibility were considered fraudulent and quickly went bankrupt.

After the advent of central banks, however, suspending convertibility became normal and was protected by government laws. In other words, central banks have become an apparatus of government theft.

The Gold Exchange Standard

> *"Shalmaneser king of Assyria came up against him, and Hoshea became his servant and paid him tribute."* — 2 Kings 17:3

As the convenience of banknotes became more popular, governments started requiring acceptance of banknotes in trade. Central banks also became common, which meant that most of the gold for each country was held in one place. These gold hoards within banks became too tempting, so governments started to take out enormous loans from these central banks. As these loans were not backed by corresponding deposits, they made central banks insolvent and fractional-reserve banking became standard practice.

For international trade, however, gold still needed to be transported because countries could not trust each other's central banks to be solvent. In the wake of World War II, most of the world's gold supply ended up in the United States under the control of the US central bank, or the Federal Reserve (a.k.a. the Fed). Largely due to this historical anomaly, much of the gold stayed in the US and every central bank other than the Fed kept dollars instead of gold in their vaults.

This was the result of the Bretton Woods agreement in 1944, which allowed non-US central banks to convert their dollars to gold whenever they wanted. Because central banks other than the Fed did not actually store gold, this was called the *Gold Exchange Standard*. The US Federal Reserve essentially became the central bank for all other central banks worldwide. In other words, the United States gained leverage over other nations through central bank domination.

This gave the United States the "exorbitant privilege" to create more dollars as long as there weren't too many countries asking to convert US dollars into gold. Though the Gold Exchange Standard ended in 1971, this exorbitant privilege, which allows the US to exchange newly printed money for goods from abroad, continues to this day. In a sense, the US is engaged in theft of the entire world—extracting a tribute from every other country like the Assyrian Shalmaneser in 2 Kings.

Conclusion

> "Can a throne of destruction be allied with You, one which devises mischief by decree?" — Psalm 94:20

Although gold-backed paper resolved many of gold's shortcomings, it introduced a fatal flaw by giving the state political control over its most important property: scarcity. Predictably, the United States created more banknotes than the gold in its vaults could justify.

This culminated in 1971 with a decision by Richard Nixon to "temporarily" suspend gold redeemability[4]. This temporary suspension has since become permanent. The dollar is still kept in central bank vaults around the world as the reserve, though it's no longer convertible to gold. This immoral decree abolished money's link to gold and placed the world on a path to financial serfdom.

This was a death-stroke to the integrity of money as it no longer was backed by anything. It brought us into the age of debt-based money that we are coerced into today—fiat currency. Fiat, or money "by decree," allows for limitless inflation. Inflation comes to us from the Latin verb *inflare* meaning "to blow up." This is an apt description since once it sets in, inflation has only one outcome historically: dilution of currency into worthlessness. On this, we have much more to say in the next chapter.

Since breaking its peg to gold in 1971, the US dollar has lost over 96% of its relative value. This is due to one of the disastrous effects of the prevailing financial system: inflation.

---

4. Source: Sandra Kollen Ghizoni, Nixon Ends Convertibility of US Dollars to Gold, Federal Reserve History

Chapter 3: Inflation

> *"Can I forget any longer the treasures of wickedness in the house of the wicked, and the scant measure that is accursed? Shall I acquit the man with wicked scales and with a bag of deceitful weights? Your rich men are full of violence; your inhabitants speak lies, and their tongue is deceitful in their mouth."* — Micah 6:10-12

HAVE YOU NOTICED that the price of basic vegetables or a gallon of milk has steadily increased over the past few years? Price increases are more obvious when they happen suddenly, like when gasoline prices spike before a hurricane. However, when prices rise steadily over time, it is accepted as normal. This phenomenon is happening for a reason and it revolves around how our money system works.

Here is a general principle to begin with: the value of money decreases when the supply of money increases. Consider how the price of food, energy, water, rent, investments, and debts are all affected by an increase in money's supply. This is classically called *inflation*. Unfortunately, over the last 70 years, the term inflation has been warped to mean the increase in prices of goods.

In this chapter, we will distinguish these two forms of inflation. The first is an increase in the money supply, which we will refer to as *monetary expansion*. The second is a decrease in the value of money, which we will refer to as *price inflation*.

Are monetary expansion and price inflation natural phenomena or manmade? And if they are manmade, who are the culprits behind these economic occurrences and what motivates them?

Counterfeiting

> *"How the faithful city has become a harlot, she who was full of justice! Righteousness once lodged in her. But now murderers. Your silver has become dross, your drink diluted with water."* — Isaiah 1:21-22

Isaiah uses the literal dilution of money and wine to illustrate a city that has become immoral, faithless, and unjust. Monetary debasement is an ancient evil, not a new notion or discovery. In short, it has always been considered theft. During Isaiah's time, people were cheating each other by adding cheaper metals to their silver. They debased their money just as the emperors would go on to do centuries later.

The difference between the people doing the debasement and the emperors doing so is that the former was illegal and the latter was legal. When the people pass cheaper metals off as silver, it is called *counterfeiting*. When the government does the same thing, it is defined in terms of the ends the government wants to achieve, such as economic stimulus or winning a war.

There have always been strong laws against the counterfeiting of money, from the death penalty in Roman times to possible lifetime imprisonment in China today. Of course, counterfeiting laws never apply to the lawmakers. To this day, governments are permitted to dilute currency; in effect, they are stealing from the community as well as from those yet to be born. God condemns this action because not only is it deceitful, it is also theft; the payor is taking value from the payee in an unfair exchange.

The Consequences of Unrighteousness

> *"For the wages of sin is death, but the free gift of God is eternal life in Christ Jesus our Lord."* — Romans 6:23

Governments who insist on dishonest weights and measures are not exempt from the biblical law of sowing and reaping. When a government sows unrighteousness in the form of stealing from its people, it reaps its own destruction.

Many books have been written about the fall of the Roman Empire, how their armies weakened, how their citizens became decadent, and how their government became more corrupt. The underlying cause of all these symptoms was monetary debasement.

After Roman Emperors had debased their currency several times, market participants that had not started anticipating the debasement went out of business. The ones that anticipated the debasement demanded more coins for their goods. The government would then debase the coins further in an economic game of cat and mouse. Ultimately, the Roman denarii became so diluted that few people even accepted it as money.

Consequently, this led to the weakening of the Roman Empire because it couldn't collect enough taxes to sustain its bloated government. The wages of sin, even for empires that last hundreds of years, is death.

Governments that expand the money supply are doing so to unfairly benefit one group over another. Citizens who receive public services from the government no longer need to work for the services, which can lead to laziness. If soldiers are paid in money that is depreciating too quickly, it can cause them to desert, leading to military weakness. Inflation is a disease on the fabric of society.

A Hidden Tax

> *"Therefore do not fear them, for there is nothing concealed that will not be revealed, or hidden that will not be known."* — Matthew 10:26

Centuries later, the biggest catalyst of the American Revolution was a disdain for unjust taxation. Disaffected colonists revolted against their British rulers for imposing higher taxes on imported tea. One of the popular slogans against these imposed taxes from the British Parliament was "No taxation without representation." During this time, there was no one in Parliament designated to speak for the wishes of the colonists. However, even though the colonists had no government representation, they were still being subjected to government taxes.

The idea of people being subject to taxation without the consent of those being governed was clearly wrong. This principle would be one of the foundational pillars by which the new American nation would structure its representative democracy.

In America, taxes are supposed to go through the legislators and be voted on by representatives of the people. Some local taxes are even voted on by the constituency through ballot initiatives. However, the most pernicious and pervasive "tax" is monetary expansion, which is enacted without legislation, knowledge, or consent of the governed. In other words, *monetary expansion*—as manifested in price inflation—is taxation without representation, or theft from the community by the government.

A tax on tea is an explicit tax. By comparison, monetary expansion is a hidden tax because it is done without consent, transparency, or legislation. This process happens in small increments, so it's hard to discern if it's happening at all. Because of its surreptitious nature, nearly every government throughout history used this hidden taxation method to fund its exploits.

We would be naive to think America is exempt from the historical constant of death by debasement. Monetary expansion consistently leads to the fall of kingdoms and empires. Why would a republic be exempt? America, too, will meet its end as it reaps the destruction it continues to sow with every dishonest measure it uses to manipulate the monetary supply.

Modern Monetary Expansion

> *"Behold, the wages of the laborers who mowed your fields, which you kept back by fraud, are crying out against you, and the cries of the harvesters have reached the ears of the Lord of hosts."* — James 5:4

We no longer use coins as our everyday medium of exchange. Yet debasement is more prevalent than ever, and the tools that governments have today are much more sophisticated and effective.

Banks issue debt out of nothing. For example, if the United States government takes in $2 trillion in tax revenue but has a budget of $2.5 trillion, the shortfall, or the *deficit,* is funded by the central bank of the US, the Fed. The Fed gives a $500 billion loan to the US government by buying its treasury bonds.

Where did that $500 billion that got loaned to the government come from? Does the Fed have depositors with that kind of money who are willing to lend to the government? It does not.

Again, the Fed creates the money from nothing. New debt is how we get monetary expansion in today's economy. In a similar vein, whenever the federal government pays back its debt, the money disappears, and we experience the opposite of monetary expansion: monetary contraction. Thus, the debt ceiling—the legislative limit on the amount of national debt the US Treasury can incur—is really just the amount of money the central bank is allowed to lend to the federal government, or how much printed money in total is allowed to exist for the federal government at any one time.

It is not only the federal governments and the central banks that engage in monetary expansion. Businesses borrowing from commercial banks can do the same thing. Commercial bonds are paid for with newly created money from the commercial banks. Even individuals borrowing from consumer banks are doing the same. A 30-year mortgage is not money from someone else's savings, but newly created money from the borrower's bank. Almost all debt in today's system is money created by banks and not savings, so nearly every loan expands the money supply.

In principle, it is possible for the amount of money in the system to shrink. In times of economic distress, more loans will be paid off than new loans made. The reduction in loans would contract the money supply, but these are precisely the times that governments borrow to fund new programs, increasing the debt level. During economic downturns, central banks lower interest rates to spur borrowing and increase the money supply. In reality, money in today's system expands continuously.

The scale of the monetary expansion is significant. One measure we can use to evaluate just how much the US dollar has been expanding is called the *M2 money stock*, which is published by the St. Louis Federal Reserve.[1] For context, the earliest data point is January 1959, when it was $286.6 billion. The M2 money stock in September 2025 was $22.2 trillion, or a 7600% increase over 66.5 years. Annualized, that is the equivalent to a 6.73% increase in M2 money stock every year.

Moral Evaluation of Monetary Expansion

> *"Bread gained by deceit is sweet to a man, but afterward his mouth will be full of gravel."* — Proverbs 20:17

When the bank loans newly created money, it is not immediately obvious who it's hurting. After all, the bank is going to earn interest on the money loaned out and the borrower has access to more money right away. The bank benefits, the borrower benefits, and it looks like a win-win for both parties.

The problem here is that the loaned money is not from someone's savings. Instead, it's created from nothing the moment it hits the borrower's bank account. The loans create extra money in the money supply. This means that everyone who has savings in this money now has a smaller proportion of its value than before.

Think of it this way. Say a bank lent out $300 trillion to the government. The government then spends the $300 trillion to build new roads, housing for every American, a spaceship to go to Mars, etc. How would that affect the community? First, since the money has been spent to pay for goods and services, all

---

1. Source: M2 Money Stock (M2), St. Louis Fed

that money enters the economy. Yet $300 trillion is more than all the US dollars that exist, so what would happen?

Everyone would start charging a lot more for goods and services. This would mean any savings people had before the new money was made would now be worth very little. In a way, the newly created money—even for something as seemingly innocent as a loan—steals from everyone who has savings.

> *"For every change of money ... involves forgery and deceit, and cannot be the right of the prince, as has previously been shown. Therefore, from the moment when the prince unjustly usurps this essentially unjust privilege, it is impossible that he can justly take profit from it. Besides, the amount of the prince's profit is necessarily that of the community's loss."* — Bishop Nicole Oresme

We need to understand that artificially increasing the money supply is theft. This was the insight of 14th century French Bishop Nicole Oresme. As his quote states above, monetary debasement is stealing from the community, and therefore morally repugnant.

Price Inflation and Purchasing Power

> *"But the Lord said to him, 'Now you Pharisees clean the outside of the cup and of the platter; but inside of you, you are full of robbery and wickedness. You foolish ones, did not He who made the outside make the inside also?'"* — Luke 11:39-40

The consequence of monetary expansion is that the prices of things go up. As mentioned above, price inflation is what people today mean when they refer to inflation. Monetary expansion generally leads to a loss in purchasing power. The US Bureau Labor of Statistics quantifies this by surveying the price of a basket of staple goods across the country every month. This is known as the *Consumer Price Index*, or the CPI.

The US Dollar has declined in its purchasing power by more than 95% since

1913. In other words the amount of goods and services a dollar can purchase has declined by more than 95% since the Federal Reserve was created.

Note that the CPI is generally less than the monetary expansion. The CPI year over year increase is around 2% while the monetary expansion is around 7%. Why are the two numbers different? If money expands by 7%, shouldn't price inflation equal 7% too? There are three reasons why price inflation doesn't track monetary expansion dollar for dollar.

First, new technologies and innovations make things cheaper. This is most obvious in rapidly changing goods such as computers or cell phones, but this is also true of goods that are slower to change, such as milk or clothes. A new chip manufacturing process might make a cell phone noticeably cheaper in a year's time. A new hormone might make cow's milk cheaper over a period of five years. A new type of tractor might lead to cheaper clothing over a period of ten years.

Second, not everything increases in price at the same rate. For example, eggs don't generally increase much in price compared to something like houses. When new money enters the economy, it generally goes toward items that preserve value well because the people spending the new money are *investing*, not *consuming*.

When prices increase, the assets that preserve value go up more than assets that don't preserve value. Stocks and real estate preserve value well, so they increase in price relatively quickly. By contrast, eggs and jeans don't preserve value so they increase in value slowly. This is why real estate prices are going up faster than the price of eggs at the grocery store. The CPI doesn't take into account the more value-preserving assets like real estate, making the price inflation look like it's less than the monetary expansion.

Third, the CPI is a heavily manipulated metric. Governments are politically motivated to show that prices are not increasing very much. After all, if prices are perceived to be increasing quickly, savings would be diminished, and the public would get upset. Several tactics have been used to manipulate CPI to show favorable outcomes.

For example, the Hedonic Quality Adjustment is a method by which the CPI gets adjusted downward. If jeans increase in price by 20%, the Hedonic Quality Adjustment can say that the quality of the jeans increased by 18% and only count that as a 2% increase.[2] This is why the CPI magically comes in at 1-3% year after year, even when prices are increasing much more in reality.

The value from technological progress should result in deflation. The fact that we have inflation means that this value is being redirected to the money creators and their borrowers. As a result, although governments report a 2% increase per year in prices, the reality is much worse. Theft is occurring right in front of our faces, and unfortunately, the community has accepted this as a normal part of life. Instead of everyone benefiting from a natural deflation of prices, we allow the few to capture all the gains.

Incentives of Monetary Expansion

> *"Either make the tree good and its fruit good, or make the tree bad and its fruit bad; for the tree is known by its fruit."* — Matthew 12:33

There is a vicious cycle created by debt and inflation. Governments want to spend vast amounts of money on social programs, wars, and many other things. When revenue from taxes is not enough to cover expenditures, they go into debt. If no one is willing to lend to the government, creating money and raising explicit taxes are the only options.

Today, governments do both. They raise explicit taxes, and they create new money by borrowing from the central bank. This causes monetary expansion, which reduces the purchasing power of the currency. Debt and monetary expansion feed on one another by mutually incentivizing the creation of more money.

When money is expanding and the interest rate is low, the economically rational thing is to maximize leverage, or take out as much debt as possible now because the debt will be worth less in the future. Since governments control the money supply, they can ensure future monetary expansion. In the current

---

2. Source: Frequently Asked Questions about Hedonic Quality Adjustment in the CPI, US Bureau of Labor Statistics

money system, all new money is debt created by banks and the interest rate on that debt is controlled by the central bank. The central bank is incentivized to create lower interest rates to lessen government debt burdens. This means there are less consequences of having debt, which incentivizes the government to borrow even more money. This is a vicious cycle.

These incentives don't just apply to governments. The entirety of society is affected. Individuals who expect monetary expansion in the future are incentivized to hold less money, or put another way, people are incentivized to consume.

Consumption of goods and services is not a bad thing in and of itself. A functional economy requires consumption, but when saving is disincentivized, debt and leverage levels rise too far, and the economy becomes more fragile. This results in the boom/bust economic cycles we are so familiar with. Financial gurus frequently tout advice like, "If you want to become wealthy, you can't just save; you need to invest." In a world of constant monetary expansion, this can be good advice, but too many people forget that "investing" involves the risk of loss.

This pressure to invest has caused a specific type of inflation that we have seen in the United States over the past decade: *asset inflation*. Asset inflation refers to the nominal price increases of financial goods in an economy: things like houses, stocks, bonds, and commodities. Because people are disincentivized from holding money, the money that would normally be saved flows into these assets, causing their values to grow at rates faster than the broader economy.

Theft of Time

> *"The plowman ought to plow in hope, and the thresher to thresh in hope of sharing in the crops." — 1 Corinthians 9:10*

Money is tied to value. Usually, we think of measuring things in various units like miles, gallons, and pounds. The units of measurement for these things don't change. One pound of wheat today is the same as one pound of wheat tomorrow. The same is not true of money. One hundred dollars today is not the same as one hundred dollars tomorrow. We don't notice or think about the reduction in value because it happens relatively slowly, but the change should not be ignored. We must pay attention to how the value of money shifts because money is the way we measure human time.

We all trade time for money in our jobs. For the average adult working a full-time (40 hour) workweek, work takes up about one-third of our time. Looking at it in this way, inflation can be described as a theft of human time and therefore, human life. The compounding effect of theft through inflation, paycheck after paycheck, year after year, prevents individuals and communities from reaping the natural benefits of technological advancement and hard work.

Unfortunately, we do not often recognize this because of the covert way inflation works. It punishes those who work hard and save. Instead of seeing their wealth grow and enjoying it or putting it to good use in the future, years go by and the time spent on hard work declines in value.

When our money is stolen, our labor is stolen. When our labor is stolen, our time is stolen. And when our time is stolen, our life is stolen. The stealing of life is what we call slavery.

Hyperinflation

> *"Therefore this iniquity will be to you like a breach about to fall, a bulge in a high wall, whose collapse comes suddenly in an instant,"*
> — Isaiah 30:13

The bad tree of inflation is known by its fruits; prioritizing consumption and the wreckage of monetary savings are just two of them. The real rotten fruit is hyperinflation, which ends in societal collapse.

The United States and the broader western world are fortunate to have mostly experienced low to moderate inflation in recent years. This is not the experience of many other countries. Since 1971, when the US abandoned the gold standard, the number of hyperinflationary episodes in the world has skyrocketed.

Price inflation is typically around 0-4% per year[3]. Hyperinflation usually indicates a rate of change in prices of 50% or more per month. Imagine going to sleep one night and waking up the next morning to learn all the dollar bills you own in your wallet, your bank, and under your mattress are suddenly worth 50% less.

All hyperinflationary episodes share the same source: governments expanding the money supply too quickly, causing the community to lose faith in the currency. Much like the verse in Isaiah where the collapse of a wall happens without warning, monetary expansion goes along until it suddenly triggers hyperinflation. No one knows what specific amount of newly created money will cause economic collapse. One day money has value, and the next day it doesn't.

Conclusion

> *"Every prudent man acts with knowledge, but a fool displays folly."*
> — *Proverbs 13:16*

We are taught that price increases are good for the economy. In fact, one of the Federal Reserve's prime directives is "stable prices," which has been defined as 2% price inflation per year. Many economic "experts" today take a negative view of deflation, which they define as a general decline in prices of goods and services. The reasoning is that deflation generates expectations for further decline in prices, causing consumers to postpone their buying of goods.

Which is better? A world where things get cheaper every year and our purchasing power increases, or a world where things get more expensive every year and our purchasing power decreases?

In a deflationary world, aided by technology, things would be cheaper to produce and a lot more affordable. People would not have to hold value in assets such as real estate. In such a world, property and other value-preserving assets

---

3. Source: Kimberly Amadeo, US Inflation Rate by Year: 1929 - 2023, The Balance

would be much more affordable. Everyone would benefit—except governments and large corporations who depend on and hold large amounts of debt.

The economic "experts" want us to plan less for the future and spend more now. The fact that governments pay these experts should give you pause in accepting their conclusions. We only need to look at history to see that monetary expansion is theft from those not in power by those that are in power.

Adding more to the money supply does not add value to the community. It only redistributes the value that already exists, paying those closest to the government first. Eventually, inflation sets in and robs anyone who cared enough to save for the future. But it doesn't stop there. If wages don't rise fast enough compared to inflation, entire future generations are robbed as they become paid less for their time.

This leads us to our next topic, the tool that makes this widespread theft possible: fiat money.

Chapter 4: The Problems with Fiat Money

> *"Those who want to get rich fall into temptation and a trap and into many foolish and harmful desires that plunge people into ruin and destruction."* — 1 Timothy 6:9

OUR CURRENT MONETARY SYSTEM is generally not well understood. What we have today is a central-bank-controlled fiat monetary system. The word *fiat* literally means "by decree." Therefore, *fiat money* describes money that is mandated by an authority. Fiat money is not backed by anything except faith in a government's decree.

This system is shockingly unjust. Its many complex layers intentionally make its inequities—and iniquities—difficult to understand. The reason for its complexity is explained well by American industrialist Henry Ford:

> *"It is well enough that people of the nation do not understand our banking and monetary system, for if they did, I believe there would be a revolution before tomorrow morning."*

Fiat money has created temptations that continue to lead us to ruin and destruction. In this chapter, we'll go over how fiat money works and why it induces corruption. In order to understand this central banking fiat money system, we must peel back several layers of complexity.

Understanding Fiat Money

> *"For they are a nation lacking in counsel, and there is no understanding in them."* — Deuteronomy 32:28

Imagine that you are a strawberry vendor at a farmers' market. A man comes up to you and offers you five purple bills in exchange for one basket of strawberries. Each bill has the number one on it, a beautiful hologram of a goose, and an embossed star.

"What is this?" you ask.

"Purple Dollars."

"Huh?"

"My buddies and I made this currency and issued it to ourselves. Now can you give me my strawberries, please?"

At this point you'd probably hand back the "money" and ask the man to pay you with something real, like US dollars. As soon as he leaves, you'd share your experience with the vendors next to you, laughing, or warning them of the crazy person who just tried to rip you off.

In reality, our modern currencies are not too dissimilar to Purple Dollars.

Why We Value the Dollar

Why do we value the US dollar more than something made up like the Purple Dollar? It is not the quality of paper or its artwork that makes the US dollar valuable. The Purple Dollar could have better artwork and be made of better-quality paper, but neither enhancement would suddenly make it more desirable. So, the question remains: why do we value USD so much more than this hypothetical currency?

THE PROBLEMS WITH FIAT MONEY

The only difference between Purple Dollars and US currency is that more people trust and believe that US dollars are valuable. In other words, USD has no value *outside of the current monetary system*. If the Purple Dollar man and his friends got into power, they could, by coercion and ultimately the threat of violence, replace USD with PD. They could make the old currency illegal and all Americans would have to turn in their USD and start using PD. The purchasing power of USD would plummet worldwide, and after a period of economic adjustment, everyone would start using the new currency and eventually forget the US dollar.

This scenario may seem far-fetched, but the Purple Dollar takeover scenario is close to the reality of how nearly every country's fiat currency became their standard currency. For instance, countries in Latin America have had many cycles of currency issuance and confiscation of both banknotes and coins. Since 1970, Peru has had two such cycles, Uruguay and Venezuela have had three each, and Argentina and Brazil have had four apiece[1].

Even without a regime change, fiat currencies tend to fail naturally. One study of 775 fiat currencies concluded that fiat currencies had an average lifespan of just 27 years, with the shortest being one month and the longest being the British Pound, which has existed since 1697. Failed fiat currencies have devastated societies as diverse as 11th-century China, Weimar Germany, France under King Louis XV, the United States during the Revolutionary War, and more recently Zimbabwe, Venezuela, and Lebanon[2].

---

1. Source: Eugenio Díaz-Bonilla, Democracy and commodity cycles in Latin America and the Caribbean, International Food Policy Research Institute
    Latin America since the mid-20th century, Encyclopedia Britannica
    Roberto Frenkel and Martín Rapetti, Exchange rate regimes in Latin America, Center for Economic and Policy Research
2. Source: The Rise And Fall Of Fiat Currencies, Dollar Daze
    Chris Thomas, The World's 12 Greatest Currency Failures, Gold IRA Guide

Why Governments Like Fiat Money

> *"Do not be among those who give pledges, among those who become guarantors for debts."* — Proverbs 22:26

When a government wants to pay off its debt, fund a war, or simply enrich itself, money is needed. Direct taxation is unpopular and often creates more problems than it solves. Cutting a nation's spending is even more unpopular, and can also create a lot of immediate problems. Printing more money, on the other hand, is cheap, easy to obfuscate, and its negative consequences generally don't show up for a while. It allows governments to quickly solve immediate problems, which appeases and reassures citizens.

Fiat money specifically reinforces existing power structures. This phenomenon is known as the *Cantillon Effect*[3]. It describes how newly printed money benefits those closest to the money supply. Such people and organizations get to acquire assets cheaply, before prices expand. Who are the beneficiaries? Banks, private equity firms, hedge funds, and large corporations.

The people that the Cantillon Effect hurts are those farther from the money creation: the poor, the politically unconnected and the working class. The Cantillon Effect also hurts future generations. The printing of money can benefit the current generation, while leaving the next generation under insurmountable debt. Millennials, for example, have come to know this personally.

Another danger of fiat money is hyperinflation, as we discussed in the previous chapter. Generally, this causes the price of goods to rise, which sets off a vicious cycle where the government prints even more money, which causes prices to go up further, and so on. As a historical and real-world example, this is what happened to the Continental Army when a fiat currency was created by the Continental Congress during the Revolutionary War[4].

---

3. Source: Nicolás Cachanosky, Cantillon Effects and Money Neutrality, American Institute for Economic Research
4. Source: Farley Grubb, The Continental Dollar: How the American Revolution was Financed with Paper Money, National Bureau of Economic Research

> *"Local merchants deny us assistance, equipment; they only take British money, so sing a song of sixpence."* — Alexander Hamilton in *"Hamilton: A Broadway Musical"*

In an effort to sustain the uphill rebellion against the British, the fledgling Congress essentially printed their currency, called *Continentals*, according to their military needs. Creating a new, untested currency, which could not yet be confirmed as enforceable through military dominance, didn't go as well as the Continental Congress had hoped. The undisciplined money printing led to the complete collapse of the Continental and brought about the phrase "not worth a Continental." This eventually led to the US Constitution explicitly requiring money to be in gold and silver.

Fiat Collapse

> *"When the money was all spent in the land of Egypt and in the land of Canaan, all the Egyptians came to Joseph and said, 'Give us food, for why should we die in your presence? For our money is gone.'"*
> — Genesis 47:15

Fiat money eventually collapses in on itself when the monetary base has expanded so much that people using the currency lose faith in its ability to properly store and transfer wealth. If central banks have the ability to directly expand the money supply without limitation, this can happen very quickly. However, in the United States and other modern fiat systems, the central banks aren't the only ones who increase the money supply. Retail, commercial, and investment banks all can and do "create" new money through loans.

Banks accept deposits and make loans with many different types of clients, including the general public and large businesses. New loans increase the money supply while repayments decrease the money supply. If the total outstanding debt stayed the same, there would be no changes to the money supply. Unfortunately, the total outstanding debt has increased year after year for decades.

Total outstanding debt has only decreased during periods of severe economic turmoil, such as during The Great Recession of 2009. The money supply contracted because banks stopped lending. Banks stopped lending because they feared new borrowers would default. As many such banks were in danger of collapse, "Too Big to Fail" emerged as an excuse for governments and central banks to prop them up. To spur more lending, central banks lowered interest rates, which caused debt levels to increase again. This increased the money supply and caused asset prices to increase, encouraging more borrowing and continuing the cycle of monetary expansion. As a result, debt levels increased even more over the following decade.

In reality, nothing is too big to fail. Eventually, societies that spend more than they produce must pay the piper. Wars, popular social programs, and political nepotism don't come for free. Debt piles up, and without fiscal discipline, the proverbial camel's back breaks.

The breaking point occurs when total debt increases so quickly that the sellers refuse to accept the degrading currency and begin to demand an alternative form of money. Hyperinflation occurs when money completely fails, as is described in Genesis when Joseph lived in Egypt during a time of great famine.

Hyperinflation is a seizure of private property by the money printer. Once a currency enters hyperinflation, the currency is no longer good, and people will hoard whatever holds value, such as foreign currency, various precious metals, collectable stamps, diamonds, and art.

Dangers of Fiat Money

> *"Yet they tempted and rebelled against the Most High God and did not keep His testimonies"* — Psalm 78:56

Numerous historians, economists, and writers have warned us of the dangers of fiat money. In Goethe's *Faust, Part Two*, the devil advises a bankrupt emperor to create money out of thin air on the promise of mining it later. The emperor is convinced and does so with the help of magicians, spiraling his kingdom into failure.

Pope Innocent IV warned against the debasement of currency without the people's approval. German philosopher Immanuel Kant warned that financing wars using debt would hurt prospects of peace. In a study of 30 currencies, economist Peter Bernholz concludes that, since 1700, there has not been a single case of a currency freely manipulated by its government—or central bank—that enjoyed price stability for at least 30 years running.[5]

Nichole Oresme, known as the "founding father" of economics, and economist Ludwig von Mises both called the inflation of fiat a "tyranny." Fiat money is immoral because it is only useful for reallocating wealth without consent. This leads to inflation, which steals our time and the time of future generations. It devalues everything individuals and communities work so hard for and incentivizes bad spending habits.

Ultimately, any future value of a community that is stored in money is being unilaterally taken by the government without the people's consent. Fiat money inevitably collapses because it misaligns incentives and allocates power disproportionately, creating an unsustainable system.

Why Fiat?

Fiat money has many negative aspects. It has no real value, a short life span, is easily manipulated, and brings the ever-present danger of hyperinflation. Considering all this, why don't governments stick with commodity-backed money? Are they ignoring thousands of years of evidence? Why have all our leaders abandoned the gold standard? Are they stupid?

No, governments know exactly what they are doing. They are practical, self-oriented, and have close ties with banks. In fact, any country that is run democratically will have politicians incentivized to create short-term economic boosts to bandage the problems of their voter base. Fiat money enables and encourages these immoral actions that sound money would prohibit and discourage.

---

5. Source: James A. Dorn, Monetary Alternatives: Rethinking Government Fiat Money, Cato Institute, p.278

If a nation is having a conflict and needs to fund a war, it can print money instead of imposing direct taxes, which would run the risk of making people question the politician's decision making. If there's a pandemic and a country wants to lockdown without immediately bankrupting their population, they can print more money. If a political party wants to get into power by promising everyone free stuff, they can execute such promises by printing money. This is the practical thing to do for any politician who desires to stay in power, because there will be no accountability for their actions. Politicians functioning under this system are no better than Faust's emperor.

Conclusion

> *"For oppression makes a wise man mad, and a bribe corrupts the heart."* — Ecclesiastes 7:7

The central-bank-backed fiat system has outrageous incentives. Print some money, lend out money that does not really exist, take egregious risks, get bailed out when things go wrong, borrow some more, and repeat. There is no incentive for governments and banks to change their behavior because it is not their labor and time that is being stolen. Value is created by real work, and the people who perform the real work are the ones paying for these excesses.

Prosperity cannot be created through money printing. Not only does history demonstrate this, but we can witness it in real-time. Some forms of money are more moral than other forms of money. Fiat is immoral money because of the ease with which it can be created and used for theft.

Until the entire monetary system is transformed from one that is based on lies to one that is based on truth, we will not escape the negative feedback loop that fiat creates.

Unfortunately, no one teaches people this reality. Instead, we invent false paradigms like "Too Big to Fail," which are designed to further perpetuate the illusion of an infallible economic system. All of this has second-order effects in the political realm, to which we now turn.

Chapter 5: Money and Politics

> *"You shall not murder.*
> *You shall not commit adultery.*
> *You shall not steal.*
> *You shall not bear false witness against your neighbor."*
> *— Exodus 20:13-16*

INFLATION AND FIAT MONEY are tools of government to steal from the community, as we've shown in the last two chapters. Yet the tools themselves are not enough. There needs to be some justification for theft and this necessitates a political philosophy.

The current central bank of the US, the Federal Reserve, was not the first US central bank. There were two central banks before it: the First Bank of the United States[1], established in 1791 after the Revolutionary War, and the Second Bank of the United States[2], established in 1816 after the War of 1812.

These central banks did not have the scope and power that the Fed does today. For example, the First Bank of the United States only had a 20-year

---

1. Source: Andrew T. Hill, The First Bank of the United States, Federal Reserve History
2. Source: Andrew T. Hill, The Second Bank of the United States, Federal Reserve History

charter and could not buy government bonds. In other words, these central banks were limited in their scope. The reason why they didn't go as far as the Fed is political philosophy.

The United States was founded on the principle that we have unalienable rights rooted in Natural Law, granted to us by our Creator. As the Declaration of Independence states:

> *"We hold these truths to be self-evident, that all men are created equal, that they are endowed by their Creator with certain unalienable Rights, that among these are Life, Liberty and the pursuit of Happiness."*

While the political philosophy of the founding fathers didn't prevent them from establishing a central bank, it did limit their ability to infringe on the economic liberties of the people. Their view was that the government was a servant to the people. A government that failed to protect its people's individual rights would lead to the people becoming servants of the government. This view of the government eventually ended the second central bank of the United States in 1836, a credit to the politicians who recognized its evil.

> *"And I sincerely believe, with you, that banking establishments are more dangerous than standing armies; and that the principle of spending money to be paid by posterity, under the name of funding, is but swindling futurity on a large scale."* — Thomas Jefferson

Generally, monetary systems that allow for theft of the community are found among governments that lust for power. Monetary systems that are not as easily controlled are found where governments serve the people and protect their individual liberties. In this chapter, we explore the role of money in politics and the spiritual origins of this economic relationship.

Lust for Power

> *"You are free to eat from any tree in the garden; but you must not eat from the tree of the knowledge of good and evil, for when you eat from it you will certainly die."* — *Genesis 2:16*

As long as there has been humanity, there has been government. Starting in the very beginning, Adam and Eve can be considered the first "government" that ever existed, endowed with the responsibility to govern over creation and rule over the earth. As the highest-ranking authorities in the Garden of Eden, Adam and Eve were not placed in the garden only for the sake of enjoying its splendor. Rather, they were tasked with cultivating their garden home. The word "work" carries the idea of cultivation, revealing God's desire for us to ensure the earth is productive and that we continue to serve as stewards of creation.

Adam and Eve were entrusted with a mission of eternal importance. They had abundance, yet they succumbed to the temptation of wanting more. They focused on the one thing that God had withheld from them. Adam and Eve took things into their own hands and attempted to play God. Tragically, governments have continued to eat from this God-forsaken tree ever since.

Those endowed with the immense responsibility to govern human societies have frequently reached for the same rotten fruit. In their lust for power and immortality, rulers have brought about their own downfalls by trying to redefine good and evil. Predictably, their decrees have enriched themselves and their inner circles while depriving the community at large.

Governments have a moral obligation to protect their citizens instead of pursuing their own agendas. These agendas may involve good intentions, such as providing safety and comfort to everyone, but as we will see, such agendas result in leaders playing god at the expense of the rights of individuals. The result is frightening, evidenced by the fact that governments over the last 100 years have been the most deadly and destructive in history.

True Justice

> "You shall do no injustice in judgment; you shall not be partial to the poor nor defer to the great, but you are to judge your neighbor fairly."
> — Leviticus 19:15

This passage from Leviticus reveals God's standard of equity and justice. Justice is intended to be blind and fair. We can neither treat people preferentially because of what they can do for us later, nor can we make excuses for people's harmful behavior. However, governments throughout the world exercise preferential treatment via legislation that favors one group over others, sowing seeds of bitterness, apathy, and division.

The above passage wasn't addressed to Moses or to the leaders of Israel, but to the entire nation of Israel. While leaders will be held to greater account, all people shoulder the responsibility of upholding justice. In the words of John Stuart Mill, "Bad men need nothing more to compass their ends, than that good men should look on and do nothing."

Justice demands that we judge individuals based on what they've done, regardless of how much money or power they have. A just monetary system enriches those who serve the community. A corrupt monetary system enriches one group at the expense of another instead of providing a fair and consistent trading environment for all.

Taking Politics out of Money

> "Absolute power corrupts absolutely."
> — Lord Acton

Money is absolute power in the marketplace. It can be used to command any form of capital. Fiat money allows governments to exist and grow without restriction. It enables limitless theft through the control of money. This is why the ability to seize the community's labor and savings is a power that no one should have. Yet because it is out there for the taking, much time, effort, and money is spent pursuing that power.

Without the ability to manipulate the money supply, politicians would be forced to explicitly tax or borrow. Inflation and fiat money, as discussed in the previous two chapters, give authorities the license to steal from the community. Putting this malevolent power of unseen theft into the hands of the government is the problem. We can't "take the money out of politics," but we can take politics out of the money. When control of money is no longer a prize, politics itself becomes less a lust for power and more about serving the community. We will have more to say on how we can take politics out of the money in chapters 8 and 9.

Government control over the money supply has many consequences, a few of which we will cover here.

First, governments are not constrained by their tax revenue. Governments can spend more than they earn and, unsurprisingly, most have racked up a lot of debt. Similarly, governments don't care much about the cost of things. Consequently, nearly every industry tries to sell to the government in one way or the other. Usually, this is done through some new government program that favors a particular industry. For example, in the United States, pharmaceutical companies have benefitted from Medicare Part D and universities have benefitted from student loan programs.

Second, governments act to preserve politically connected companies and industries—even if these companies are outdated and uncompetitive. Generally, this takes the form of bailouts or the nationalization of certain industries, particularly banks and insurance companies. Newly printed money is used to prop up companies that would normally go bankrupt. In other words, there is a strong bias towards preserving the status quo, protecting those in power.

Third, higher interest rates incentivize people to save while lower interest rates incentivize people to spend. Because governments tend to be debtors, central banks are incentivized to keep interest rates low. Since savings are stolen through inflation, there are less savings in the economy in general. Less savings means that people are much more vulnerable to economic shocks, causing even more dependence on government generosity. Furthermore, less savings means more spending and consumption, the consequences of which we will explore more in the next chapter.

The government's monopoly in the market for money is an absolute power that corrupts absolutely. The result of a debt-based fiat monetary system is that governments become willfully unjust by stealing from the people to benefit themselves and their friends.

Good Intentions and Unlimited Budgets

> *"For the word of God is living and active and sharper than any two-edged sword, and piercing as far as the division of soul and spirit, of both joints and marrow, and able to judge the thoughts and intentions of the heart."* — Hebrews 4:12

Many politicians try to do the best they can for their constituents. Improving schools, building new infrastructure, or expanding social programs look attractive on the surface. The problem is that each program requires a lot of money.

Politicians constantly compete for a share of the government budget so they can fund the desires of their voters. When money has limits, this competition can lead to positive outcomes where the most important projects receive funding. A constrained budget prevents spending money on frivolous and/or costly endeavors.

On the other hand, when the budget is limitless, politicians can double down and not have to admit any mistakes. Why debate what to fund when you can print money at will and fund it all? Spending money that isn't yours is easier than spending money you earned; making this action limitless is a sure path to destruction.

In 1917, the US Congress passed the Second Liberty Bond Act, which imposed a budget restraint called the debt ceiling. Before 1917, there was no debt ceiling in force, but there were congressional limitations on the amount of debt that could be issued by the government. This debt ceiling was effective while our money was backed by gold. Gold acted as a natural constraint on government spending.

As explained in Chapter 2, the United States government ended the direct convertibility of dollars to gold in 1971 and the US Dollar became a fiat currency. This removed the natural constraint of gold's scarcity on debts and created the current political situation of using more money to cover up old spending mistakes.

Consequently, political issues now get evaluated on intentions and not on results. Government budgets get corrupted by payments to politically connected people under the guise of well-intentioned programs. For example, consider the Department of Education and the Department of Energy. The first intends to increase the quality of education and the second intends to reduce price volatility in energy markets. Since these departments have been created, neither has made progress on their intentions, but their budgets have favored constituencies such as unions and large companies.

The debt ceiling was intended to limit government budgets, but politicians continually vote to raise the debt ceiling in order to fund various projects. They have voted over 60 times to raise the debt ceiling since 1971 and the massive runup in government debt reflects this undisciplined spending. In other words, the debt ceiling has been completely ineffective. As a result, the world teeters on the brink of financial collapse every 10 to 15 years.

How many politicians have been allowed to double down instead of admit error as a result of fiat money? Ultimately, these politicians will have to answer to God as Hebrews says.

More Money, More Problems

> *"For he who does wrong will receive the consequences of the wrong which he has done, and that without partiality."* — Colossians 3:25

New government debt is effectively new "money." Every dollar the government borrows eventually makes its way into the world as it is used to pay for goods and services. This seems great on the surface. As goods are purchased, companies make money and employ more people.

As discussed in Chapter 3, however, this is an illusion since the borrowed money was effectively stolen from the community. All that economic activity is essentially funded by value stolen from the savings of everyone holding the currency. Value that would have been saved or spent based on the individual's or community's desires instead gets spent by the government.

As explained in Chapter 3, progress is deflationary. Consider the massive deflationary force of technological progress. As technology improves, production costs are driven down, and we are able to produce more goods and services for less. For example, the mobile phone has progressed dramatically to the point that a current generation iPhone is a camera, calendar, video phone, music player, television, gaming device, and health monitor all in one. A device with equivalent features in 1991 would have cost a fortune!

Even with this technological innovation, the general trend in prices has been inflationary. As we pointed out in Chapter 3, the difference between natural deflation and observable price inflation is value being stolen from the community by the money printers.

In regions such as South America, Eastern Europe, Southeast Asia, and Africa, the effects of inflation have been more pronounced. The people living in those regions have routinely felt the despair and hopelessness of this monetary manipulation. In other regions of the world, monetary manipulation has shown itself in other forms such as massive increases in wealth inequality, which is driven by asset inflation.

The Origins of Wealth Inequality

> "Truly, truly, I say to you, he who does not enter by the door into the fold of the sheep, but climbs up some other way, he is a thief and a robber." — John 10:1

A growing political issue all over the world today is wealth inequality, and for good reason. The rich are getting richer, seemingly without doing much at all, while the majority of people struggle to stay out of debt. Younger generations are especially affected as evidenced by the fact that they don't have as much wealth as their parents did at the same points in their lives. Meanwhile, the older generations are having to delay retirement because the wealth they thought they had has dwindled away. Essentials such as food, housing, and healthcare are getting more expensive. This is not a sustainable situation.

Many have acknowledged this problem and there have been endless suggestions on how the government can solve it. Universal healthcare, college debt forgiveness, and universal basic income are just a few of the political proposals. These suggestions attempt to address the *effects* of growing wealth inequality, but they fail to address the *underlying causes*.

One of the underlying causes is that the government can spend newly created money on whatever sector of the economy it wants. The government isn't particularly price sensitive because it can print new money to fund its spending. Such indiscriminate spending generally doesn't add value to the community.

Since the printed money is stolen from one group of people, and the money spent is going to another group of people, this is just a form of wealth redistribution. Keep in mind that whenever wealth is redistributed, it must go through many different channels first, where it gets diluted amongst middlemen. Wealth moves from taxpayers and savers to government contractors. It is not a coincidence that many government contractors are fabulously rich.

Besides this obvious political cronyism, there is another way in which money flows towards the politically connected. Even if the government is getting good value from some expenditure, there is the Cantillon Effect, which we touched on in Chapter 4. In our current system, rich people have access to very low interest rates, which are enabled by new money printing. This allows them to purchase assets more inexpensively than someone who has to deal with higher interest rates.

For example, during the Global Financial Crisis of 2008, housing prices collapsed. Homeowners couldn't afford their mortgage payments and owed more than the houses were worth. The government bailed out banks and kept them afloat, while homeowners sold for a loss or got foreclosed on. In the meantime, politically connected groups got low-interest loans to purchase these distressed assets. They were able to sell at a massive profit a few years later and got even richer.

Such shady deals are only possible because of the control of money by the government. Much like the thief that climbs in some other way, many of the rich have obtained their wealth through theft. Money printing by the state bestows riches on the favored, which leads to expanding wealth inequality.

Marxism and Money

> *"The fool has said in his heart, 'There is no God,' They are corrupt, and have committed abominable injustice; There is no one who does good."* — Psalm 53:1

Growing wealth inequality attracts people to political philosophies that sacrifice individual rights for a collective vision. Marxism, Communism, and Socialism are three such political philosophies whose injustice is hard to overstate. The notion that capital can be collectively owned for the benefit of the community is at the heart of these ideological illusions.

In reality, administrators of this "collectively owned" capital confiscate it for themselves. Collectivism contradicts accountability. With over 100 million lives and counting in the past 100 years, these political philosophies have caused more death and destruction than any other by the abuses of leaders such as Mao, Stalin, and Pol Pot. As Communism, Socialism, and Marxism all share Marxism at their roots, we'll be using the word Marxism to refer to all three from here on.

> *"Religion is the opium of the people."* — Karl Marx

As this quote from Karl Marx reveals, Marxism is atheistic at its core. It is less known that a debt-based fiat monetary system is a necessary weapon for its political program. The fifth plank of the Communist Manifesto reads: "Centralization of credit in the hands of the state, by means of a national bank with state capital and an exclusive monopoly."

Karl Marx wrote this in 1848, well before central banks became popular. As mentioned in the previous chapter, the devil in Goethe's *Faust* creates wealth for the prince through the abomination of fiat money. Marx was well known to have loved Faust and he often recited large portions of the devil's dialogue from memory. Marx believed in central-bank-backed fiat money and he was literally inspired by the devil from *Faust*.

The moral depravity of Marxism is obvious to anyone who has studied history. It is a system that is in and of itself immoral, no matter what type of money is used. By facilitating theft from the community and undermining property rights, fiat money is one of the core enablers of Marxist policy which aims to capture private property for the benefit of the state.

Once the community's assets and freedoms are captured, unfathomable abuses of power have occurred, resulting in the murder and starvation of millions during a very small span of history.

The Illusion of Something for Nothing

> "For false Christs and false prophets will arise, and will show signs and wonders, in order to lead astray, if possible, the elect."
> — Mark 13:22

Despite its moral bankruptcy, Marxism and its related political ideologies can appear attractive. During times of economic difficulty when the abuses of the political system run rampant and basic needs of the populace go unmet, a political philosophy based on sharing everything—especially resources from the rich—sounds great. Free government services, such as healthcare, education, and housing, seem like things that would balance the rampant corruption being facilitated by politicians and bankers.

Such sentiments are lust for power in disguise. Two wrongs do not make a right, and promises for free government services almost always benefit some politically-connected rich individual and not the people who are actually in need. The promises of a government "for the people" are typically lies, meant to bring a new set of people to power. Advocates promise that the new government will finally be a servant of the people, but reality often shows that they're just the new masters, not much different from the old masters.

The problem is the power is centralized. The solution to the abuse of power isn't to bring in new managers for this weapon of community theft, but to remove this tool of control altogether. Sadly, those that would be our new masters deceive many, much like the false prophets Jesus warned us about in the Book of Mark.

Taxing the Rich and Modern Monetary Theory

> *"But that slave went out and found one of his fellow slaves who owed him a hundred denarii; and he seized him and began to choke him, saying, 'Pay back what you owe.'"* — Matthew 18:28

Another popular solution of Marxist origin is to heavily tax the rich in order to pay for government services. Such sentiments sadly misdiagnose the root of wealth inequality. With an ever-expanding fiat currency, taxing the rich in an effort to address wealth inequality is like using thimbles to bail water from the Titanic. Like the slave shaking down a fellow slave for a hundred denarii when there's a debt of ten thousand talents, taxing the rich at even 90% would not be enough to pay for a small portion of the country's deficit.

The latest Marxist proposal is called *Modern Monetary Theory*, or MMT. MMT speculates that government deficit spending is good so long as prices don't get out of control. According to MMT, prices can be controlled through taxation. Since both monetary policy and taxes are within the control of governments, this approach is presented as an economic cure-all. The problem is that MMT depends on politicians never making mistakes. Under MMT, politicians pick the winners and losers.

History shows that allowing the free market to sort out success and failure is a superior option. When the economy isn't pumped full of fiat and interest rates aren't artificially lowered, depressions tend to be short. Unfortunately, these non-events are not mentioned in history books. For example, the stock market underwent a depression in 1920-1921.[3] Federal spending was cut instead of increased, and the federal government left the market alone unlike its counterpart in the 1930s—which resulted in The Great Depression. The market, in other words, corrected itself and didn't need massive intervention. Unfortunately, examples like "The Depression of 1920-1921" are rarely remembered.

Essentially, MMT is an excuse for more government spending. The

---

3. Source: Grant, James (2015), The Forgotten Depression: 1921: The Crash That Cured Itself, Simon and Schuster

justification for printing money is to provide services for the underprivileged and to combat growing wealth inequality. As explained in chapters 3 and 4, deficit spending by governments expands the money supply, which steals value from the community. Therefore, the benefits are illusory, essentially robbing Peter to pay Paul.

No value is being created through this wealth redistribution scheme. MMT is just another justification for theft of the community by the government, couched in the language of justice to make it more palatable.

The Violence of Fiat Money

> "But you said in your heart,
> 'I will ascend to heaven;
> I will raise my throne above the stars of God,
> And I will sit on the mount of assembly
> In the recesses of the north.
> I will ascend above the heights of the clouds;
> I will make myself like the Most High.'"
> — Isaiah 14:13-14

Lust for power, like most vices, has no bounds. As ambitious authoritarians complete the subjugation of their own citizens, they start eyeing other countries for conquest. Much like Lucifer's ambition in the Book of Isaiah, lust for power is a major reason for war.

War is also very expensive. The government has to pay for weapons, soldiers, training, and transportation. Historically, many wars ended when one side ran out of money. The losing side, and sometimes the winning side as well, finished with depleted resources, lots of debt, and no one willing to lend them any more money. Essentially, wars were mostly paid for with a limited and somewhat quantifiable amount of a country's hard-earned cash reserves.

Before the 20th century, the government could only use the resources it could pay for. Fiat money eliminated this restriction and introduced an unfortunate power grab by the government. When new money can be created with little effort, the resources of the community are more easily usurped for the war effort.

For example, fiat money enabled a continual escalation that resulted in an unnatural extension to the global devastation of World War I. The participants of WWI were still nominally under the gold standard, but they got around it by suspending convertibility. Once banknotes were no longer convertible to gold, each central bank was allowed to print banknotes at will, expanding the money supply. Money printing allowed all the participants of WWI to continue the war without normal financial limitations. By printing money, each country could direct the resources of their populations toward war.

Without the limitation of hard money, there was nothing to stop the complete devastation of entire communities, a situation seen in both world wars. Fiat money turned limited war into total war and brought about so much more death and devastation than in times past.

Today, the permissiveness of modern central banking enables ongoing expansion of the *Military Industrial Complex*. When fiat money can be created so easily, the government is incentivized to invest in its own preservation by bolstering its military's capabilities, even in times of relative peace. Look no further than the various wars the US has engaged in to see that this is the case.

Conclusion

Governments continue to be ruled by fallible humans who lust for power. They take for themselves the "forbidden fruit" made available by fiat money. As long as governments continue to create fiat money, they will be playing God. As we have learned from Adam and Eve, playing God leads to death.

Governments become more corrupt the more that power is centralized. Centralized control of money is an immense political power that has been used for unprecedented evil. Throughout history, leaders have shown that they are not good at resisting the temptation of hidden and instantaneous mass theft. Neutralizing this tendency requires money that is not under the control of the government, or anyone else.

Government corruption is not the only bitter fruit being harvested from the current monetary system. Bad systems corrupt our character. They influence how we act, permeate our relationships, and affect our life choices. These moral implications are what we turn to in the next chapter.

Chapter 6: The Moral Consequences of Corrupt Money

> "They promise them freedom, but they themselves are slaves of corruption. For whatever overcomes a person, to that he is enslaved."
> — 2 Peter 2:19

THE POLITICIZATION OF MONEY, inflation, and fiat money allow governments and certain privileged individuals to reap where they did not sow. This disincentivizes productive, valuable work and instead incentivizes theft of all kinds. Money was intended to store the value of work across time, but it has become the prime tool to exploit the community. The consequences of these sins are significant. In fact, they impact almost every aspect of life. This chapter explores a collection of moral attitudes and spiritual malaise that are the bad fruits of bad money.

Fiat's Treadmill

> *"Set your minds on things above, not on earthly things."*
> — Colossians 3:1

Inflation in our current monetary system demands ever-increasing sacrifices from the community. To preserve wealth in an inflationary economy, a large investment of time, energy, and even money is required. Consider the prevalence of financial services such as professional investing, tax accounting, and retirement planning. These are all mechanisms that, among other things, attempt to outrun inflation. None of these "wealth advisory services" existed as professions under the gold standard; there was no need for them.

Like a treadmill that requires a lot of effort to go nowhere, broken money requires everyone who wants to preserve the value of their wealth to constantly work. The more wealth a person has, the more time, energy, and money they need to spend on wealth preservation. A reasonably wealthy person can expect to spend a significant amount of time researching stocks, mutual funds, real estate and other investments to beat inflation.

On the other end of the spectrum, the poor depend on debt. Due to their lack of income and assets, poor people are burdened with higher interest rates. This makes repayment more difficult, creating even more dependence on debt. This cycle of debt is devastating emotionally, psychologically, and relationally. Poor people are forced to spend an inordinate amount of time and energy either trying to avoid this cycle of debt or attempting to manage that cycle of debt once they've gotten mired in it.

At all levels of wealth, money has become a primary driver of many life decisions. What job should I take? How many kids should I have? Which political party should I support? Such decisions are often made through the hazy lens of dishonest money. Where God's eternal purpose for our lives was supposed to provide insight and guidance into all consequential life decisions, now money occupies a much larger part of our lives than it otherwise would. In other words, we are pressured to trust money more than God.

It's Just Business

> *"You shall have just balances, just weights, a just ephah, and a just hin; I am the LORD your God, who brought you out from the land of Egypt."* — Leviticus 19:36

In this verse from Leviticus, God demands a fair and accurate exchange, one that gives as much value as it receives. A trade pleasing to God benefits both parties of the exchange.

Fiat money creates an environment where people want something for nothing. It is money that encourages wealth redistribution instead of wealth creation. This makes the ethics of trades irrelevant to the average person, encouraging a "win at all cost" mentality.

Those who are trusting of others in the economic realm are seen as gullible and often taken advantage of. With the fiat money system in place, the focus is no longer on ethical trades, but on getting ahead. This imbalance leads to a fundamental erosion of society by sowing seeds of distrust.

This societal erosion is perhaps most obvious in the use of the phrase, "It's just business." The phrase is used to justify all manner of unrighteous behavior. Ethical boundaries are hastily crossed in order to win exchanges to the point where the baseline for ethics is no longer recognizable. Sadly, this is seen even among Christians dealing with one another.

> *"One whose heart is corrupt does not prosper; one whose tongue is perverse falls into trouble."* — Proverbs 17:20

Dishonest money puts the focus on winning the exchange, instead of creating mutual value for both parties. Bad money incentivizes ripping people off even if we don't like to think of it that way. We justify our actions by subscribing to a worldview which normalizes unjust behaviour in the realm of money. Our lack of understanding of the current monetary system has made us slaves of money.

Too Big to Fail

> *"For what does it profit a man to gain the whole world, and forfeit his soul?"* — Mark 8:36

Inflationary money incentivizes undisciplined spending, but what happens when there isn't any money left to spend? In our current monetary system, the solution is to go into debt. Debt is everywhere and at every level of society. Consumers take on credit card debt, corporations issue bonds to raise capital, and large hedge funds use complex debt instruments.

As the past few financial crises have shown, our system isn't as robust as our leaders claim. There are many over-leveraged banks, companies, and individuals out there, some so large that they are designated as "Too Big to Fail." Such companies take on substantial risk because they can fall back on government bailouts should their bets go wrong.

This risk dynamic creates massive confusion among market participants in terms of how to best evaluate risk and how to allocate money and effort. In addition, the moral hazard created by bailouts makes such companies bloated as they operate in inefficient ways because they become less price sensitive. In short, they do not care how much they spend or how far into debt they go, because they are confident the government will eventually bail them out. This is where we are now.

A company that receives a government bailout has a clear competitive advantage over its rivals. Bailouts help the ailing company, but also hurt its rivals, especially small businesses that do not receive the same government support. Such a system is not free market capitalism, but corporatism. Favored companies can collect profits to enrich themselves but can socialize their losses to the public.

Undisciplined Risk-Taking

> "In the morning sow your seed, and at evening withhold not your hand, for you do not know which will prosper, this or that, or whether both alike will be good." — Ecclesiastes 11:4-6

In the Parable of the Talents, a master gives three of his servants an amount of money fitting to their abilities. The first two servants invest the money and produce returns. The third buries the money and gives his master back the same amount that he had received. In other words, he takes zero risk and gets zero reward. His master is dissatisfied; after all, he could have easily buried all his money himself. The third servant let him down with his lack of action. This story makes clear that prudent stewardship is one of our God-given responsibilities.

By contrast, a bailed-out company has an advantage that it neither earned nor deserved. In the current system, loans have a rate of interest far below what it would take to borrow the same amount from someone with savings. This is because the money for those loans cost nothing to create *as they come from nothing*. As a result, there is an escalating game some large companies are "playing"—that of going into debt in order to take greater and greater risks. This makes such companies increasingly fragile to unexpected events such as the 2008 mortgage crisis or the 2020 coronavirus disaster.

The kind of risk taking that is incentivized by bailouts is undisciplined. Instead of being prudent stewards who make the most out of every resource, bailout recipients use their funds to forestall the consequences of bad decisions. They are throwing good money after bad.

Increased Rent-Seeking Behavior

> *"For we hear that some among you are leading an undisciplined life, doing no work at all, but acting like busybodies. Now such persons we command and exhort in the Lord Jesus Christ to work in quiet fashion and eat their own bread."* — 2 Thessalonians 3:11-12

Rent-seeking is a tax on a transaction that a middleman collects without adding value. Whereas work is value-additive, rent-seeking is value-subtractive. Picture a bureaucrat who makes no clear contribution to society. Rent-seeking behavior is an ancient practice, as the passage from 2 Thessalonians shows. The passage calls on the busybodies, who are rent-seekers, to work and provide value.

Fiat money is the fuel for exponential government and bureaucratic growth. This creates a lot more space for rent-seeking behavior. The presence of a central bank distorts the risk and reward for certain occupations and industries. In a bad money system, the compensation for work is no longer based solely on the value provided to the community. Work compensation is also highly dependent on how close the industry is to where the money is being created.

Our current system creates many rent-seeking opportunities throughout the economy. The ratio of university administrators to professors has grown exponentially since 1971 because of subsidies from student loans and additional compliance requirements. These jobs exist to comply with the government instead of supplying value to the market. Since the money supply was expanded to pay such people, value is stolen from the community. This is why rent-seeking is a form of theft and should be condemned.

Not only is this type of work unhealthy for the economy at large, but it is unhealthy for the individual employing such practices. Meaningless work causes deep spiritual distress. Meaningful work provides value to the community and satisfies the soul.

Commerce Before Community

"And we are writing these things so that our joy may be complete."
— 1 John 1:4

The obsession with money has created an undue dependence on commerce over community. It's not a coincidence that we don't know our neighbors on the same level as previous generations. Ironically, this tends to be even more true in heavily populated areas like cities. We are social beings, but worship of money has made us into cohabiting strangers.

This has far-reaching effects on not only our communities but ourselves in our personal relationships with each other and with God. We can't truly worship God without loving our neighbor. The glue of any community is the duty and obligation we have toward our neighbors, so it's no surprise that the worship of money destroys community.

In a bad money system, the care for the old, underprivileged, and downtrodden is too often outsourced to the government. This takes away individual responsibility, and a displacement of charity occurs. We live in a system that conditions us to feel that as long as the taxes are being paid, the "widow and the orphan" will be taken care of. Individual virtuous action is overtaken by the feeling that voting for government programs is just as helpful. We're effectively being told that we don't have to care for our neighbors. In reality, such programs have failed time and again because, unsurprisingly, it is hard to be effective at helping others when the foundation is built on theft rather than on charity.

In our current monetary system, the government can claim to "solve" nearly any problem by creating a new program funded through debt. As discussed in Chapter 3, the printing of new money doesn't create new resources. Expanding the money supply in a fiat money system is theft. Therefore, solving one set of problems for one group of people always creates problems for someone else. In other words, government programs are not charity, but theft. The wealth redistribution through inflation is not voluntary and helps one set of people while injuring another.

Think again of the law of sowing and reaping. If we do not invest time, energy, and resources into our neighbors, we cannot expect to cultivate peaceful, interdependent communities. Under our current monetary system, the fiat treadmill reinforces divisive narratives that continually paint our neighbor as our enemy who must be defeated, outperformed, or voted out of office.

This condition has had a detrimental effect on society as a whole because people are more focused on *money* rather than on *each other*. When communities are so transient, it becomes difficult to get to know our neighbors, so we give up on trying. After all, what's the point of learning their names when they are just going to move in a year or two?

Something for Nothing

> *"For which of you, desiring to build a tower, does not first sit down and count the cost, whether he has enough to complete it?"*
> — Luke 14:28

The fiat fiasco of the last hundred years has fostered mass denial among politicians and the public alike. Look no further than claims of "Too Big to Fail" during the Great Recession as evidence of the widespread refusal to own up to our abysmal economic reality.

Our current monetary system is a debt-based system, one where new money is created through issuance of new debt. This debt is available at all levels, from the US government, through issuance of treasuries, to consumers, who are issued new short-term debt through credit cards or payday loans. Somewhere in between are mortgages, car loans, student loans, and corporate bonds.

In an honest monetary system, all debt represents money that someone else has invested. That is, the money is coming from someone's real savings and the person lending hopes to share in the profit of a specific venture. In our current system, most debt is just freshly printed money. It comes from nothing. An honest money system is one in which invested savings always exceed debt. Our current system definitely does not fall into this category.

Consider the difference between borrowing money that a lender worked hard to earn versus borrowing money that a lender simply printed out of thin air. The latter is perhaps the most salient example of blatant rent-seeking behavior.

How many people would lend someone hundreds of thousands of dollars at 3% over a 30-year term with a house as collateral? Almost none, because few have that much saved up, and those that do would want more than 3% and would not be willing to wait 30 years for a return. Few, if any, savers would rationally lend out money at this rate from their own hard-earned savings.

Banks do this all the time. They can do this because they are not sacrificing anything. They are getting something (interest) for nothing, which is money created out of nothing. The beneficiaries are the bank, the borrower, and the seller, but everyone else in the community pays through their own savings being diluted. The borrower gets a very cheap loan relative to the free market. That means the borrower can afford something much more expensive, especially because the term of the loan is so long. As a result, housing prices increase, which is a form of asset inflation as discussed in Chapter 3.

In an honest money system, individuals would use deflationary savings to purchase assets, and the assets would not be driven up in price. More people would be able to afford a home, while taking on less long-term risk. This is why the average home price has increased from two years' worth of average wages to six years, and one share in the S&P 500 has increased from 20 hours of average wages in 1980 to 165 hours in 2025.

Modern Debt Slaves

> *"Owe nothing to anyone except to love one another; for he who loves his neighbor has fulfilled the law." — Romans 13:8*

The benefits of debt to the borrower are not without cost. The debt is with the borrower until it's repaid in full, with interest. During that time, the borrower is shackled by the obligation and the debt itself becomes a form of enslavement.

Society is drowning in so much debt that it has been normalized. Yet most people understand that debt isn't a good thing, and in many households it's a significant source of stress. Debt causes people to work, not at what they like or are talented in, but in what pays the most. Ethical considerations of taking a job, making a profit, or even working the job itself are often disregarded because of the urgency of debt repayment. We become enslaved to debt to the point of money being the major factor in just about all of our decisions.

Debt also has a negative impact on the condition of our relationships as servicing the debt supersedes our innate human desire to invest into the people who are closest to us, both with our time and resources. More and more, debt has become the ruler over our lives and has taken the time that should be devoted to our families, communities, and God.

Dehumanized Work

> *"Whatever you do in word or deed, do all in the name of the Lord Jesus, giving thanks through Him to God the Father."*
> — Colossians 3:17

The rise of massive corporations and governments that employ thousands of people and control vast swaths of the economy is exacerbated by fiat money. Organizations are able to swell to enormous sizes thanks to the Cantillon effect. For example, multinational conglomerates have access to cheap debt that isn't available to the average small business owner, and they have the ability to grow much bigger than they would without that cheap source of capital. This means that companies and governments are able to grow far beyond what would be possible in a competitive free market.

The larger the organization, the more difficult it is to have accountability. Issues such as *regulatory capture* arise, where the very bodies that are supposed to serve the public by regulating an industry instead serve the interests of the industry, due to misaligned incentives. For example, a regulatory body like the FDA that is supposed to make sure food production isn't contaminated instead allows all sorts of abuses. This is usually due to industry-lobbied legislation and bribery in the form of former regulators being hired for large sums after their stint in government.

As a result of cheap debt, regulatory capture, and large-scale operations necessary to produce profit, organizations grow to enormous sizes and tend to dehumanize their workforce. Employees go from being familiar faces to rows on a spreadsheet.

These conditions can lead to a deep bankruptcy of the human spirit, especially when work merely provides enough money to survive and to service debt. People become debt slaves, merely executing the commands of masters, spending their most productive hours working on someone else's assets. This poisons and perverts our outlook on work.

We're not even "gaining the world" as we are forfeiting the future. When everyone is up to their eyeballs in debt, we are all a crisis away from complete and utter ruin. Given such vulnerability, it is no wonder our society today has record levels of anxiety, depression, and suicide.

Materialism

> "If the dead are not raised, 'Let us eat and drink, for tomorrow we die.'" — 1 Corinthians 15:32

The opposite of saving is spending. Spending is greatly incentivized in an inflationary economy. This is because money is decreasing in purchasing power and worth less in the future. In other words, an inflationary currency is like a giant game of reverse musical chairs; whoever is left holding the money when the music stops, loses.

What we call materialism today is really a desire to live it up now at the expense of tomorrow, or what economists call *high-time preference* behavior. In a sense, people in fiat money societies end up devaluing the *later* part of their life in exchange for a better *now*. The virtue of prudence, or *low-time preference* behavior, has been lost to us, and it has profound effects at a societal level.

In the United States, upwards of 80% of people live paycheck to paycheck[1]. A community that doesn't plan for the future devolves into chaos; a community

---

1. Source: Zach Friedman, 78% of Workers Live Paycheck to Paycheck, Forbes

that plans does much better. Bad money creates less incentives to plan for the future. Additionally, investing for the long term is made difficult because of the unpredictability of bad money. Saving is punished through inflation and the alternative, investing, is a whole job unto itself. Spending, living it up, eating and drinking without regard to tomorrow can seem more rational, especially for those without talents in investing.

Bad money deprives the community of hope for tomorrow. Tomorrow becomes less predictable and less worth saving for. Paul's admonition that hope in the resurrection is an essential part of Christianity underscores the point. Our hope for the future is what leads us to plan and work and not just indulge in worldly pleasures while we still can.

Good money allows the community to plan effectively, incentivizing saving and giving us a reason to have hope for the future.

Degraded Quality of Goods

"Your silver has become dross, your wine has become diluted with water." — Isaiah 1:22

Isaiah is talking about the debasement of silver, which had become more polluted and less pure. The wine in this case had also been diluted. These two things are directly related. Over time, as money degrades, products on the market also degrade. As explained above, consumers in a fiat system tend toward materialism, or high-time preference behavior. They are more willing to pay for goods now rather than later because of price inflation.

They are also more willing to accept lower quality goods because they don't care as much about the good's long-term value. This means that sellers have a lower bar of quality to meet. Naturally, this causes sellers to degrade the quality of their products to make more profit.

As prices inflate, sellers have a strong incentive to keep their own product prices the same, even as the money they receive degrades. This is because consumers generally hate it when prices go up. This phenomenon is what economists call *sticky prices*. The costs for their labor and supplies tend to go up, so to compensate, suppliers degrade their product. Often, they degrade their products gradually to make it harder for consumers to detect. For example, Tropicana orange juice containers have shrunk from 64oz in 2000 to 46oz in 2025 while the price has increased from 2.99 to 4.99.

Another option to combat price increases is to scale to get better prices producing in bulk. This is a factor in why companies are so large in our current monetary system. Since scale is required to combat the effects of inflation, small businesses that focus on quality are often priced out.

Finally, sellers can lower their costs by optimizing. They reduce costs by sourcing cheaper components, reducing manufacturing overhead or optimizing the supply chain. None of this necessarily reduces product quality, but there is a significant temptation to cut corners on things the consumers won't notice. For example, an egg manufacturer might give the chickens cheaper feed, which keeps the eggs looking the same, but degrades the egg's nutritional value. Sadly, this temptation of cutting corners is too much for most sellers to resist and that results in more degraded products.

Debased money leads to debased goods and debased goods are how civilizations slowly self-destruct. The sins of our monetary system are leading to the corruption of goods and, ultimately, to the death of our community.

Conclusion

Bad money has led to spiritual malaise. Our current monetary system is full of systematic sins. It incentivizes dishonesty, rent-seeking, dehumanizing work, and theft instead of quality goods, strong communities, and hard work. Bad money corrupts our work, our purpose, our relationships, and our communities.
Unfortunately, the Church has also been stained by bad money, and we discuss this in the next chapter.

Chapter 7: How Bad Money Corrupts the Church

> "As obedient children, do not be conformed to the passions of your former ignorance, but as he who called you is holy, you also be holy in all your conduct." — 1 Peter 1:14-15

THE MODERN WORLD is ruled by passions. The love of money has its grip on most people, including many professing Christians. Love of money motivates people to lie, steal, betray, and abuse. People use their lust for money to justify sins of all sizes. They allow the gain and loss of money to steer their lives, and the unfortunate truth is that bad money infects the Church in the same way that bad money infects people.

This should be no surprise since the Church is made up of people. If people are obsessed with money, this attitude will spill over to the Church. How does that play out in regard to how the Church functions today? When it comes to finances, what are churches doing that they shouldn't be doing? Can we, as the Church, do anything to guard against the pitfalls that corrupted money brings?

In this chapter, we'll look at the different ways in which the Church is affected by bad money systems and what the Church can do to combat the effects.

The Breaking Point for Martin Luther

> *"Why do you look at the speck that is in your brother's eye, but do not notice the log that is in your own eye?"* — Matthew 7:3

Concerns about money in the Church are not new. Every church would like more money to do more of God's work and see the lack of money as a major limitation of their ministry. The desire to do God's work is good, but coveting money for that reason is not.

A perfect example of this is when the Roman Catholic Church began monetizing *indulgences*. Indulgence is a practice from the Roman Catholic Church to reduce the penalty of sin by performing penance. Starting in the 12th century and culminating in the 16th century, indulgences could be bought by a generous donation. They took the form of printed letters, with an area left blank where the purchaser could sign their name.

Indulgences started out as an aid to penance but ended up as a tool of enrichment for the entire Catholic Church. This system was especially abused by Friar Johann Tetzel, who is credited with issuing indulgences for not just living Christians, but also for their dead relatives. "When a penny in the coffer rings, a soul from Purgatory springs," Tetzel was known to say. Tetzel's exuberant act of greed was the breaking point for Martin Luther, the Catholic responsible for starting the Protestant Reformation.

Churches, in other words, have not been immune from rationalizing unrighteous behavior in order to gain financially. We tend to view this period of church history with condescension. We ask, "How could anyone think that paying some priest could help you repent for your sins?" We may even dismiss its significance as a typical pre-Enlightenment blunder.

However, these self-righteous conclusions are looking past the log in the eyes of our present-day churches. Are churches today much different than they were back then?

Debt-Laden Church

> "And if you lend to those from whom you expect repayment, what credit is that to you? Even sinners lend to sinners, expecting to be repaid in full. But love your enemies, do good to them, and lend to them without expecting to get anything back. Then your reward will be great, and you will be children of the Most High, because he is kind to the ungrateful and wicked." — Luke 6:34-35

The scriptures can at times be difficult to interpret. As a result, there are very few points where one could find something approaching universal consensus among Christians in all times and in all places. And yet the historic attitude toward debt is one of few such areas. Throughout both the Old and New Testaments, debt is repeatedly portrayed negatively. Debt is said to enslave (Prov. 22:7) and endanger (Prov. 22:26-27).

God repeatedly states throughout scripture that he desires his people to work and generously share the fruit of that labor (Psalm 37:21). Debt inhibits such generosity. Debt declares that one doesn't have what they need, whereas God promises to provide for the needs of His people (Deut. 15:6). Even in the few places where God permits indebtedness among his people, he also commands that there be strict limits into how long such indebtedness should last (Lev. 23:1-15, Deut. 15:1).

Perhaps most pointedly, God used the image of debt to describe both the consequences of sin and the action that Christ undertook to save us. God repeatedly reveals himself as one who sets captives free, as the forgiver of debts so that people might be free to carry out his purposes in the world.

It's astonishing, therefore, to see how comfortable so many churches and Christians have become with debt. And while it is far from the heart of the matter, the fiat money system described in the previous chapters has only served to exacerbate the problem.

Perhaps the most obvious consequence of central-bank fiat money is that loans are plentiful. As covered in Chapter 3, money is continuously expanding, and banks are in a constant search for good borrowers. Unsurprisingly, many churches are in debt, usually because of mortgages they've taken out on their big, beautiful buildings.

The rationale for buying buildings is easy to understand. We can do so much more ministry! We can get more people to join our community! We can save on rent and build equity instead of wasting God's money! We can save so many more souls! All of these arguments have some element of truth to them, but where is that money coming from?

Usually, mortgages on church buildings are paid out from the church's future revenue. As with any other kind of business venture, banks evaluate church revenues through pledges and offering receipts as the basis for receiving approval for a loan. The receiving of the loan means future congregants are essentially paying later for a new building now.

Churches that do this are imitating the habits of governments in deficit spending. While asking God to forgive their spiritual debt, they take on financial debt. The money borrowed by the church is like most other loans. It is created out of nothing by the bank.

As discussed in Chapter 4, the obvious beneficiaries of the loan are the bank and the borrower, but what is not obvious is how this dilutes the community's savings. In a fractional reserve system, every new loan adds to the inflated money supply, so churches that borrow are expanding the money supply and stealing value from the community. Besides the theft from the community, the church is saddling future members with debt. Is this the path to righteousness? Is this what Christ would want for His Church? How does God judge this?

Servants of Money

> *"The rich rule over the poor, and the borrower becomes the lender's slave."* — Proverbs 22:7

Getting into debt is an existential risk for a church. The church becomes a servant to the bank as the above verse in Proverbs states. Because loans are so readily available to churches, many have bought or built buildings that they wouldn't otherwise be able to afford. If enough tithing congregants leave, churches can get in major financial trouble, which can be destructive to their testimony and dampen their ministry.

Initially, this shows up as an accounting deficit, which requires cutbacks to the church budget, which can cause even more people to leave, leading to more cutbacks. This cycle can cause a slow and torturous death for many churches. As a result, the pressure for many of these churches is to keep as many tithing congregants as possible because losing them could trigger a downward spiral.

Another possibility is an undue emphasis on alternative revenue, such as renting the church out for other purposes and even selling some of the real estate. Churches involved in such practices function more like landlords or real estate speculators on behalf of the banks they owe debt to. They become more focused on debt service, instead of ministry, which is another way of saying that they become slaves to their lenders.

While the intentions to take on the debt were meant for good, intentions are not enough. Debt has paved a path of unrighteous practices that have little or nothing to do with spreading the Gospel.

Country Club or Church?

> *"I hate your new moon festivals and your appointed feasts,*
> *They have become a burden to Me;*
> *I am weary of bearing them."*
> *— Isaiah 1:14*

This passage in Isaiah shows that we can have correct outward actions, but if our hearts are not right, God will not accept our sacrifices. How many churches have really examined how they've stewarded their financial resources? How many churches are just religious country clubs?

The same economic pressures that cause companies to go into debt also apply to churches. Churches compete with one another for tithing congregants and that means having nicer facilities and programs, which cost money. A church that is spending more will likely be able to attract more members. In other words, the emphasis on keeping a large number of tithing congregants causes churches, especially large ones, to be very consumer driven.

This can have a warped effect on how the church measures its success, by the size of the congregation and the revenue that comes with it. The result is predictable: churches emphasize satisfying congregants and their financiers instead of pleasing God. Churches start to look more and more like country clubs instead of mission-driven communities.

For example, churches may establish a budget based on what will attract the most people instead of what will honor God. Besides their lavish buildings, there's high quality furniture, state-of-the-art A/V equipment, delicious snacks, and a host of musicians. When adding congregants is the name of the game, many churches measure their success on that basis alone.

This misalignment of priorities also leads some pastors to preach in a way that appeals to the most people possible with popular topics like spiritual gift inventories, dealing with loneliness, and parenting techniques. Calls to repentance from sin are de-emphasized or foregone altogether.

In some ways, churches imitate our political system, where politicians focus on getting votes, which also takes a lot of money. Sometimes truth and popularity will coincide, but more often than not, the Gospel gets contaminated or watered down.

Of the World

> "I have given them Your word; and the world has hated them, because they are not of the world, even as I am not of the world. I do not ask You to take them out of the world, but to keep them from the evil one. They are not of the world, even as I am not of the world. Sanctify them in the truth; Your word is truth. As You sent Me into the world, I also have sent them into the world." — John 17:14-18

In the garden of Gethsemane, Jesus was wrestling with the burden of facing an agonizing death. In the middle of the worst possible stress, Jesus prayed for His friends and the future Church. As believers, we have been sent into the world, yet we are not to be "of the world." That is, we are not to share the world's priorities, methods, and goals. We are to see the world through God's eyes, and that means acknowledging that, many times, God's ways and the world's ways do not align.

Money is one of the means by which the world tries to make the church "of the world." Churches in the U.S. receive all sorts of tax benefits along with exemptions from local zoning laws. Donations are tax deductible, giving church revenue an advantage. There are even government programs like the Paycheck Protection Program Loans, which gave $7.3 billion to religious organizations in 2020.

Shouldn't we count the cost of these "benefits" the Church receives? What is the price that the Church pays for these provisions that the state grants? The most obvious price is compliance and obedience. Many churches will helpfully comply with government mandates without a second thought because of their reliance on the government's handouts. Churches don't dare criticize their local governments anymore.

Implicitly, the line between Caesar and God becomes blurred and obedience to God gets intermingled with obedience to the state. In other words, churches become indistinguishable from any other organization, doing the bidding of the State and not doing the will of God.

Prosperity Gospel

> *"And Jesus said to His disciples, 'Truly I say to you, it is hard for a rich man to enter the kingdom of heaven.'"* — Matthew 19:23

The lure of material wealth is obvious in how many prominent megachurch pastors and tele-evangelists get caught embezzling. Jimmy Swaggart is one example, misappropriating $158 million during his ministry. A quick online search for "pastor steals from church" will reveal an array of shameful cases ranging from a couple of thousand dollars to millions, often used for personal expenses like luxury cars.

The unrighteousness of these actions is obvious, but the love of money has led to a more indirect assault on the gospel, embodied by a movement within the Church popularly known as the *prosperity gospel*.

The so-called *prosperity gospel* is the theology where congregants are told that benefits in this world—such as material wealth and good health—will come to them if only they have enough faith which is shown by financially supporting the church. Parishioners are encouraged to place their focus on any financial troubles or health issues they're having and to "seed" their faith in being redeemed from these woes by making a financial contribution.

The advice in Luke 6:38 to "give and it shall be given...pressed down, shaken together, running over" is interpreted to mean worldly material wealth instead of spiritual growth. The prosperity gospel is particularly attractive in a money-obsessed world because it is the worship of money clothed in the worship of God. It should be obvious to any discerning believer that this is a twisting of the Word.

The main issue with the prosperity gospel is that it has made faith transactional. People have taken to selling the work of their church using sermons that sound more like multi-level marketing pitches than a sharing of the Gospel—all to encourage donations. Indulgences have been rebranded in this modern era, except this time they're not selling forgiveness of sins. They're selling material wealth.

The inverse of the prosperity gospel could be found in places like the USSR, where the churches that continued to function took the opposite extreme of promising salvation through poverty. Those with little to give were encouraged to give it all, hurting themselves and their families, while enriching corrupt churches. This was the result of communism poisoning human behavior.

Both systems hold an undue focus on money. Overly materialistic societies framed money as a benefit of salvation. Contrast this with Communist Russia, where money was demonized. The poor were exploited with the promise of salvation through further poverty. These approaches are two sides of the same coin. The Church should be aware of and condemn such perverse teachings.

The Love of Money

> *"For the love of money is a root of all sorts of evil, and some by longing for it have wandered away from the faith and pierced themselves with many griefs."* — 1 Timothy 6:10

The Bible contains over two thousand verses about money. Although money itself is never condemned, loving money is. We can love any type of money, but if the system is set up in a way that encourages people to always want more, to get more, to spend more, the love of money grows too.

If the system is set up so that we feel entitled to wealth—especially someone else's wealth—then money will be more likely to corrupt our character. And if our economic system allows some of our largest institutions to steal without repercussions, then the morals of the surrounding society will decline. Whenever we are playing a game where everyone cheats, we will be tempted to cheat.

If churches do not acknowledge the immorality of debt-based systems of money, then they will ultimately participate in them. We cannot rise above something we do not name. The immorality of fiat money and the financial structures of debt are not even acknowledged, let alone seriously considered or condemned. As the obsession and love for money goes unchecked in the body of believers, the Church will reap a harvest of unrighteousness.

As we discussed in the last chapter, the debasement of money and the debasement of morals are interrelated. By encouraging a return to a solid monetary foundation, the Church can help the world move past corruption so the world can hear the fullness of the Good News.

Condemning Immoral Money

> *"You are the salt of the earth, but if salt has lost its taste, how shall its saltiness be restored? It is no longer good for anything except to be thrown out and trampled under people's feet."* — Matthew 5:13

God has sent the Church into the world to be both salt and light. Why did he use those two metaphors?

Salt was the primary way that meat was preserved in the ancient world; it allowed meat that would otherwise go bad within days to provide nutritional value to people weeks or even months later. It does this by forming a hard, protective covering around the entire surface of the meat.

What does light do? Foundationally, light gives information. It illuminates our surroundings and reveals the things around us.

It may feel radical for a church to denounce the way most of the world functions, but this is precisely what Jesus did. The story of Jesus persists as the most powerful and recognizable narrative throughout the world. Even the secular world is dominated by Biblical language in its stories, morals, laws, and measurements of time. If the goal is to improve the moral foundation of money, we must look to God, no matter how radical it seems.

Faith in Jesus means faithfully following Jesus, and it's not always easy. Trying to live out the Sermon on the Mount, for example, is hard work. Commitment, intentionality, and humility are much more laborious than listening to a 45-minute sermon once a week. The Fruit of the Spirit is not cultivated through a transactional belief. Love, joy, peace, patience, kindness, goodness, faithfulness, gentleness, and self-control grow from within as a disciple of Jesus, who points us to God through his imitable life.

The proof of salvation is not on a piece of paper issued by a central authority, but in whatever fruit is present. Or as Jesus put it, "They will know you by your fruit," and also, "A good tree does not bear bad fruit and a bad tree does not bear good fruit."

The Church has an opportunity and a responsibility to become increasingly aware of its indulgence in the corrosive fruit of bad money. This will require humility, repentance, and righteous action. We must reclaim the moral high ground and not just debate and posture.

The church must literally, urgently, and tangibly embrace its divinely ordained obligation to call humanity forward, by helping people articulate the problem of our corrupt money with precision and clarity. When we declare with conviction that our current monetary system is corrupt from a position of spiritual and moral authority, we begin to participate in bringing people closer to God. This means leaders of churches must flee from the superficial and materialistic level of economic understanding that defines today's culture.

Conclusion

> *"And He made a scourge of cords, and drove them all out of the temple, with the sheep and the oxen; and He poured out the coins of the money changers and overturned their tables ..."* — John 2:15

We have access to more wealth, information, and innovation than we've ever had before, yet the world continues to be engulfed by chaos. It seems that with every problem we fix, new problems arise to occupy the vacant slot. What is the Church to do when facing such a daunting moral duty?

Perhaps we are at the part of the story where Jesus marches into the temple and flips over the tables of the moneychangers. Today, that means exiting the corrupt fiat economy and preparing for the flood that is sure to rise. The world cannot continue to endure the recurrent economic collapses ushered in by the debt-based fiat money system.

So, how can we prepare for this? How can we, the Church, be more moral when it comes to money? In the next chapter, we present what we believe is the superior moral alternative to our debt-based fiat money system—Bitcoin.

Chapter 8: Bitcoin, a More Moral Money

> *"The Lord's bond-servant must not be quarrelsome, but be kind to all, able to teach, patient when wronged, with gentleness correcting those who are in opposition, if perhaps God may grant them repentance leading to the knowledge of the truth, and they may come to their senses and escape from the snare of the devil, having been held captive by him to do his will."* — 2 Timothy 2:24-26

IT HAS BEEN SAID that you can judge the importance of an idea by the vehemence of its opposition. In the sixteen years since its inception, Bitcoin has been called many things—a scam, a fad, tulip mania 2.0, the Myspace of money, the Model-T of cryptocurrencies, libertarian idealism, Magic Internet Money, the biggest bubble in history—but in the context of the history of money, Bitcoin is a giant leap forward.

Bitcoin is a form of money that is new in substance, security, and transparency. More importantly, Bitcoin is both a leap forward in the technology of money and a return to moral money.

In Chapter 1, we mentioned that money is a tool, and that tools never emerge out of a vacuum. Tools always arise as a specific response to a particular problem or need. Bitcoin is no different.

At Bitcoin's inception, anonymous creator Satoshi Nakamoto included a message that read as follows: "The Times 03/Jan/2009 Chancellor on brink of second bailout for banks."

Satoshi's words were written in the context of the Great Financial Crisis of 2008. Satoshi was directly referencing the carnage and injustice that the modern economic system had unleashed on millions of people. When the dust settled, five trillion dollars' worth of pension money, real estate value, bonds, 401(k)s, and savings went up in smoke.

Several hundred thousand hours of work disappeared in a few weeks. In the US alone, millions lost their homes and millions more lost their jobs. Meanwhile, the banks and politicians that intentionally allowed and personally benefited from the morally bankrupt system received millions of dollars in bonuses.

In the wake of 2008's economic destruction, Bitcoin is showing the world there is a better way. Bitcoin was created to redeem the good aspects of modern money while restoring money to its original goal: serving and helping mankind, not destroying it. The free market creation of money settled on gold as its optimal tool, but gold was ultimately corrupted by central banking. Bitcoin has the potential to serve as the redemption of money.

Some have tried to downplay the significance of Satoshi's message, but when you look more closely at what Bitcoin does, then Satoshi's condemnation of the current monetary order becomes difficult to deny. In other words, getting rid of the corruption of the current monetary system was part of Bitcoin's design and purpose. In this chapter, we lay out what Bitcoin is and why it is particularly suited to redeem the corrupt monetary system.

An Alternative to Bad Money

> *"Do you not know that when you present yourselves to someone as slaves for obedience, you are slaves of the one whom you obey, either of sin resulting in death, or of obedience resulting in righteousness?"*
> — *Romans 6:16*

We cannot understand Bitcoin's significance without understanding that our money is broken. It is much easier to grasp a thing's importance after understanding the need it fulfills. This is why many people remain uninterested in Bitcoin; they don't realize there's a problem to be fixed.

The previous chapters focused on the problems of the current monetary order. We showed that the monetary systems we live under are at best naïve, and at worst, based on lies and theft. As we've discussed throughout the book, bad money enables theft, corruption, laziness, and intemperate behavior. More importantly, bad money tempts us to worship money. If bad money is at the root of these problems, good money, or a money that incentivizes moral behavior, is what we should turn to.

Before we continue this chapter, keep in mind that this book is focused on the moral consequences of Bitcoin. Therefore, we won't be addressing the technical aspects in detail. If you are interested in those details, the Resources section at the end of this book offers plenty of places to learn more about Bitcoin. Note that learning about an entirely new monetary system is not a small undertaking and will require some time and effort to understand. For the rest of this chapter, we will describe the properties of Bitcoin and their moral consequences.

What is Bitcoin?

Bitcoin is money that is digital, decentralized, and scarce.

Bitcoin is *digital* as opposed to physical, meaning it is native to computers. Bitcoin can be sent directly to someone else, much like handing an envelope of physical cash to a friend, except over the Internet.

Bitcoin is also *decentralized*. Bitcoin does not come from, nor is it controlled by, a centralized source. This is because Bitcoin does not need a trusted authority to function. There is no bank or credit card company that acts as an intermediary. Bitcoin is built on 100% verification, and 0% trust.

Digital and decentralized might not seem like much at first, but believe it or not, that specific combination did not exist for money until 2009 when Bitcoin was introduced.

Lastly, Bitcoin is perfectly scarce, having a 21-million-unit limit. There can never be any more than 21 million Bitcoin. We'll explore how this is enforced later in this chapter, but first, let's look at the problems that Bitcoin solves.

The Problem of Trust

> *"Do not trust in princes,*
> *In mortal man, in whom there is no salvation."*
> — Psalms 146:3

Computers and the Internet have made a lot of things in the world much more efficient. They have enabled us to shop from home, communicate with people from across the globe, and follow events from anywhere. This is in part because digital objects are extremely convenient. Unlike physical objects, digital objects can be copied perfectly and near instantaneously. For example, making a copy of a book in digital form is significantly faster and easier than making a copy of a book in physical form.

Digital objects are easy to copy, and that's a big problem if we want to limit the quantity of digital objects. For instance, when you "send" an email, you are actually sending a copy, as you still have the email in your sent folder. Similar problems exist with music and movie files.

Until Bitcoin, the only way to limit the quantity of digital objects was to designate an authority. For instance, if you buy a book for your Kindle, Amazon keeps track of the fact that you paid and gives you access to the book. Amazon, in this case, is considered the *trusted authority* between you and the publisher of that book.

The existence of a trusted authority makes the exchange much easier. In our case, both you and the publisher can trust Amazon. Otherwise, the publisher would have to set up their own credit card fraud department and e-reader system and you would have to evaluate the publisher's legitimacy and solvency. Given how popular Amazon is, there's a good chance that both you and the publisher have trust relationships with Amazon already, making the transaction less prone to fraud on both sides.

Unfortunately, trusted authorities like Amazon add their own problems.

For example, if Amazon decides to take away your book, they can. This is no theoretical problem. They have done this in the past with books they decided they no longer wanted on their platform. If Amazon deletes your account, you may not have access to anything digital you bought from them. Technically, you don't really "own" your digital book as much as you have access to the book with Amazon's permission. In other words, the trusted authority has its own chance to commit fraud.

The US dollar operates the same way. The trusted authority may be your bank, Visa, PayPal, the Fed, or any number of financial intermediaries. We don't really "own" the money in those accounts. We just have access to the money with the trusted authority's permission. For example, many credit cards will not allow you to buy expensive sneakers followed by gasoline within a 30-minute window. Why? Many stolen credit cards have the specific pattern of buying those two items, so buying them in that order is prohibited.

Trusted authorities can be problematic because they can abuse their power. Anyone who has had to deal with getting money to missionaries in certain foreign countries knows how difficult that can be. This is in large part because of the many intermediaries that the money has to go through. As most money in the world today is moved digitally, the trusted authorities have an outsized say in who gets to move money around and who doesn't. In many instances, these trusted authorities steal from transactions, either by demanding bribes or by adding extra fees.

Solving Trust

> *"For every breach of trust, whether it is for ox, for donkey, for sheep, for clothing, or for any lost thing about which one says, 'This is it,' the case of both parties shall come before the judges; he whom the judges condemn shall pay double to his neighbor." — Exodus 22:9*

Bitcoin removes the need for a trusted authority. Bitcoin can be transferred directly, much like exchanging physical cash, but done over the Internet. A trusted authority is not needed because there is a complete record of every transaction that anyone can download. This ledger is called the *blockchain*, and anyone can check for transactions directly. Using cryptography, any computer or cell phone can verify the legitimacy of any transaction.

Unlike a silver piece that's been debased or a gold coin that's been clipped or a hundred dollar bill that's been counterfeited, Bitcoin is extremely difficult to fake. Its authenticity can be checked quickly and easily on a low-end mobile phone. Because Bitcoin is so easy to verify, it's less susceptible to fraud like counterfeiting.

Unlike the arbiters of the financial system, Bitcoin cannot be bribed because there is no central authority. In other words, Bitcoin makes transactions much easier to trust and is thus a more moral alternative.

The Problem of Inflation

> *"A faithful man will abound with blessings, but he who makes haste to be rich will not go unpunished."* — Proverbs 28:20

As covered in Chapter 3, fiat money's main problem is that its supply can be inflated to oblivion. This expands the supply of the currency, making it less valuable over time, deterring people from sound long-term financial planning and saving. As covered in Chapter 3, monetary expansion is a way for government authorities to steal from the community through a hidden tax, usually without representation, legislation, or transparency.

The reason this theft is possible is because of the existence of a central bank. A system of money without an authority that can expand the money supply wouldn't have this problem. In other words, a more moral money wouldn't have a central money-printing authority.

As covered in Chapter 2, traditional money already existed in nature, like salt, seashells, and silver. These all have the property of decentralization, or the lack of a central money creator. As long as these goods were difficult to acquire, they functioned well as money.

For this reason, gold is a more moral money than paper. Central banks can always print more money and steal from the community in a fiat money system. In a gold money system without any fractional reserve banking, an equivalent amount of theft would be much more difficult to pull off.

Solving Inflation

> "Better is the poor who walks in his integrity than he who is crooked though he be rich." — Proverbs 28:6

Bitcoin and gold are both decentralized in a similar way. Unlike fiat money, there is no single producer of Bitcoin just as there is no single producer of gold. The production of Bitcoin is costly, much like the production of gold. Yet anyone with a computer can try to mine Bitcoin just as anyone with a shovel can try to mine gold.

Bitcoin is superior to gold in that the total supply of Bitcoin is already known. Bitcoin is the only money in the world that exhibits *absolute scarcity*. There will only ever be 21 million Bitcoin in existence. This differs from gold, which continues to expand in supply via mining. In 2019, NASA found an asteroid with a million times more gold than all the gold that exists in the world's vaults. If gold could be cheaply mined on such an asteroid, gold would go the way of salt or seashells and no longer be used as money.

The scarcity of Bitcoin is guaranteed in a way that gold is not. Bitcoin is therefore a more just money, one that is resistant to theft by central bankers as well as technical innovations and discoveries.

This predictable, transparent, and immutable supply gives Bitcoin a significant advantage as it competes for the trust of the community to become a reliable store of value. Unlike government money or even gold, people know with absolute certainty that Bitcoin will never have its value compromised by an unexpected supply increase. Bitcoin's fixed supply also provides a fixed measurement of value which encourages consistent quality and disincentivizes cutting corners.

Put simply, Bitcoin is non-inflatable money in a world where wealth is continuously stolen by inflation.

The Problem of Confiscation

> *"You who preach that one shall not steal, do you steal?"*
> — Romans 2:21

Unless you're burying gold in your backyard, storage of personal funds is neither private nor secure. Trusted authorities such as banks can and do seize money for a variety of reasons—some justified, some not. Illegal activity like money laundering is an example of what some consider to be a "just" reason for a bank to confiscate an individual's money. An example of an unjust reason would be the 2013 Cyprus bail-in, in which depositor funds were confiscated overnight.

Monetary abuses are usually the result of major economic failures, government power grabs, and civil unrest. India's ban on large bills in 2016 is another such recent case. Confiscation of this kind results in life savings being stolen overnight. Monetary abuses such as these are theft by the authorities. The theft is often due to a lack of fiscal discipline.

Perhaps no act in recent history was quite so brazen as executive order 6102 by Franklin Roosevelt in 1933[1]. The order seized gold from everyone in the United States. Gold had to be turned in for $20.67/oz. Soon after, gold was re-priced to $35/oz by legislation in 1934. The executive order was a ploy to give the government more money to spend without explicit taxation. As in the Cyprus and India incidents, executive order 6102 was one of many where the governing authorities stole from the community through confiscation.

Solving Confiscation

Confiscation is easy to enforce only when all of the money is in one place. While executive order 6102 applied to all gold, including that which was privately

---

1. Source: Gary Richardson, Alejandro Komai, Michael Gou, Roosevelt's Gold Program, Federal Reserve History

held, the main targets of the order were banks, where the gold of millions of depositors could be seized at once.

How did we end up with all these banks being giant repositories of money? The main reason is historical. As discussed in Chapter 2, the physical nature of commodity money means that it is difficult to secure. Security is difficult enough that most people delegate this responsibility to experts, like banks. The downside is that the money is all in one place and it's much easier for governments to steal from the community.

Bitcoin is digital, so security isn't dependent on armed guards and thick steel doors. Bitcoin wallet software, which is the digital equivalent of a physical vault, is much less costly and easier to set up. As a result, everyone can be their own bank, making unjust confiscation much harder.

The Problem of Censorship

> "And he causes all, the small and the great, and the rich and the poor, and the free men and the slaves, to be given a mark on their right hand or on their forehead, and he provides that no one will be able to buy or to sell, except the one who has the mark, either the name of the beast or the number of his name." — Revelation 13:16-17

Governments today use the regulation of money to control people. Many laws have some financial component to them, such as applying pressure to comply via threats of fines or jail time. If a government doesn't like certain types of commerce, certain types of people, or even certain countries, they penalize banks and corporations for servicing them. This is what is known as *financial censorship* and it is akin to what the beast in Revelation is engaging in—restricting all commerce to only those that have its mark.

Once again, the ability to restrict certain transactions only exists because there is a financial intermediary. Banks, credit card companies, PayPal, and Venmo all have restrictions on whom you can pay. This is because, for governments, penalizing these intermediaries is a lot easier than punishing individuals. The natural result is that transactions that have the potential of being unlawful often get censored.

This may sound fine when government motives are just, but is problematic when they are not. Censoring payments to terrorist organizations is one thing, but censoring donations to missionaries is another. The regulation of the intermediary is fraught with temptations for any government. Though most censorship of transactions is meant to be good, such intermediation is used for political favors, cover ups, and extortion.

Solving Censorship

Bitcoin is running on tens of thousands of computers around the world and, as a result, there is virtually nothing that any government can do to affect its operation. For instance, if the Japanese government banned Bitcoin, all the computers running the Bitcoin software outside of Japan would remain unaffected, and even users in Japan would still be able to transact. It is fairly easy for anyone to run Bitcoin software, so it's unrealistic for governments to succeed in shutting down all instances of it.

Morally speaking, censorship is a tricky topic. Once the power of censorship is in place, it is very likely that it will be misused in the future. Censoring evil transactions might be a useful tool for a government, but historically that same tool has been used to censor transactions of political opponents, whistleblowers, dissidents, religious groups, and more.

Bitcoin, because of its lack of central authority, allows morally good and morally evil transactions between consenting parties. Much like the presumption of innocence, it is more moral to allow the freedom to transact. This is the same standard we use for paper cash.

Criticism

Bitcoin has a mixed reputation, largely because of how some bad actors have used it, particularly in darknet markets. For example, many darknet markets use Bitcoin as a payment method for drugs, pirated movies, and hacked personal data. Bitcoin has also been used as a payment method by ransomware, which is a class of computer viruses that encrypt personal files and hold them hostage until a payment is made.

Bitcoin has undoubtedly been used as a payment method for hush money, bribes, and worse. This is often the only thing the media reports concerning Bitcoin, while ignoring the vast amount of cash that is also used for similar transactions. Certain things are made easier by Bitcoin, largely because of the lack of a financial intermediary, but that's also Bitcoin's strength.

Just as Bitcoin has been used for bad purposes, Bitcoin has been used for good purposes. Many people fleeing the Maduro regime in Venezuela have been able to flee with whatever little wealth they have left. They can't use cash or gold because physical money is more likely to be stolen or confiscated. Instead, they sell whatever possessions and money they have for Bitcoin before crossing the border.

Similarly, people living under oppressive regimes in places like Afghanistan, Turkey, and Nigeria are able to store their value instead of having value stolen by their governments who are inflating their respective currencies. Many people working abroad are able to use Bitcoin to send money home to their families at a fraction of the cost of corrupt cross-border money transfer systems. People in many third-world countries are able to buy goods they otherwise couldn't get because credit cards and PayPal aren't available in their countries. People have used Bitcoin to donate anonymously to causes that may be politically unpopular or have negative consequences to their job security should their employers find out.

These are two sides of the same coin. Bitcoin does not have an intermediary, which can be both good and bad. A financial intermediary has all sorts of new opportunities to do evil. With all the different moral temptations that we've examined, we believe Bitcoin's lack of censorship is more moral and superior to its alternatives, including the current debt-based fiat money system.

Price Volatility

No discussion about Bitcoin would be complete without at least mentioning the price. Bitcoin has been the target of a lot of speculative investment since 2010. The fact that Bitcoin has gone from pennies to over $100k per Bitcoin obviously has something to do with that. The volatility has attracted a lot of traders and the price appreciation has attracted many speculators.

Bitcoin's volatile nature has also been the subject of many headlines. Additionally, the volatility and speculation are facts about Bitcoin, and this has the potential to inflame greed and recklessness. Given that we live in a culture that worships money, Bitcoin has the potential of becoming part of the problem.

The reason for the volatility has to do with Bitcoin's adoption. Price volatility is normal when markets attempt to discover the true value of an asset and tends to subside as the asset's value grows. The price of Bitcoin reflects how much people trust it. That trust waxes and wanes with time, but it increases over the long term because of Bitcoin's history and monetary properties. The fact that Bitcoin is the highest performing asset class in history is evidence of this accrued trust.

Altcoins

There are literally thousands of alternatives to Bitcoin that have popped up since 2011. These "cryptocurrencies" have all sorts of interesting names like Ethereum, Ripple, Bitcoin Cash, and Tron. Although they are all different, the single common characteristic is that they are *not* Bitcoin. In fact, most of these altcoins are outright scams trying to take advantage of the enthusiasm that exists for Bitcoin.

The chief quality of Bitcoin—true decentralization—is missing from altcoins, which all have some sort of central foundation or founder that acts as a trusted authority. Unlike altcoins, Bitcoin has rules that are not subject to the control of a central authority.

Most of the benefits of Bitcoin outlined in this chapter don't apply to altcoins. For this reason, altcoins don't deserve consideration as a superior moral alternative.

Conclusion

Bitcoin, at a technical level, is hard to steal, easy to verify, and impossible to inflate. Bitcoin takes the power out of the hands of financial intermediaries and gives sovereignty back to users. Bitcoin allows individuals, as opposed to institutions, to hold and be responsible for their money. Bitcoin removes the biases and temptations of human intervention and replaces them with inviolable and transparent computer code.

Under Bitcoin, governments can't steal from the community through a financial intermediary or a central bank. Bitcoin allows more trust in transactions, trust in value holding over time, trust in security from confiscation, and trust in not being censored.

Bitcoin is a money and a system all in one, resolving both the technical and moral issues that plague the alternatives. We can think of Bitcoin as software that is superior to gold and automates away the need for central banks. Bitcoin creates a completely different monetary ecosystem, one that doesn't have the immoral incentives of a central money printer. Bitcoin is a system that turns our individual sinfulness into our economic salvation. Bitcoin converts our individual self-interest into good for the community. As the Russian philosopher Solzhenitsyn said:

> "If there are to be salvific revolutions in our future, they must be moral ones—that is, a certain new phenomenon, which we have yet to discover, discern, and bring to life."

These are the things that make Bitcoin unique and important, and if we don't waste the opportunity, Bitcoin could enable a completely different economy: a moral one.

Chapter 9: The Redemption of Money

> "If anyone builds on this foundation using gold, silver, costly stones, wood, hay or straw, their work will be shown for what it is, because the Day will bring it to light. It will be revealed with fire, and the fire will test the quality of each person's work." — 1 Corinthians 3:12-13

NOTHING EXISTS IN ISOLATION. Everything is interconnected and money is a major source of those connections. The form of money we use affects everything we do. Bad money incentivizes immoral behavior, immoral behavior builds up immoral systems, and immoral systems lead to failing civilizations. Given how corrupt and liable to theft our current monetary system is, it is no surprise that it is a terrible foundation on which to build.

How do we redeem the monetary system? What would it look like? What would change and how do we get there? In this final chapter, we lay out a vision of what a community on a Bitcoin standard looks like, and how it could come about.

Bitcoin Adds Accountability

> *"If we turn to God and come face to face with him, we must be prepared to pay the cost. If we are not prepared to pay the cost, we must walk through life being a beggar, hoping someone else will pay."*
> — Bishop Anthony Bloom

The word accountability comes from the same word as accounting. *Accountability* is the "reckoning of money received and paid." It is reaping what you sow. The founding father of accounting, a Catholic Friar named Luca Pacioli[1], created the concept of double entry bookkeeping, where every credit matches every debit. He translated a clear set of ethics into a formula that represented a practical reality, as well as a moral aim.

As we have demonstrated in the previous chapters, honest systems of accounting have long been violated. In other words, *our modern monetary system has not been held accountable.*

It's easy to feel like victims, just trying to get by while those with power make bad decisions. When we conduct ourselves as though our actions have no consequence, then we are not victims, but a reflection of the corrupt system.

Bitcoin is a system with strict accountability. Unlike the current monetary system which violates accounting rules through theft, Bitcoin requires a matching of inputs to outputs, debits to credits, and spending to revenue. Bitcoin programmatically adds moral constraints that fiat money does not. A world on a Bitcoin standard, therefore, would be a different place with different incentives.

---

1. Source: EAA admin, Luca Pacioli: Father of Accounting, Everything About Accounting

Better, Smaller Government

> *"I passed by the field of a lazy one, and by the vineyard of a person lacking sense, and behold, it was completely overgrown with weeds; its surface was covered with weeds, and its stone wall was broken down."* — Proverbs 24:30-31

The larger the government, the less accountable it is, and fiat money enables unbridled government growth. Inflation is used to fund public programs, which results in bigger regulatory bodies. An economy based on lies and theft will fund programs based on intention and not results. Intentions, after all, are much easier to sell.

As virtuous as the intentions may be, results are rarely evaluated. Consequently, ineffective programs proliferate. Since results don't matter, nepotism and corruption thrive. In other words, money stolen from the community is spent frivolously. Fiat money incentivizes us to throw money at every problem, which increases the size of the government but does nothing to address underlying problems.

Bitcoin changes this. The power of stealth taxation through inflation is removed as an option. Adherence to a specific budget naturally constrains the growth of bureaucracy by forcing programs to compete with each other for resources. This competition ensures that, over the long term, only the most creative and effective programs survive. Such constraints also limit cronyism and grift.

Governments generally don't acknowledge their mistakes or willingly shrink, so they need boundaries imposed on them. A government constrained by a Bitcoin standard would have to answer for its actions and wouldn't be able to surreptitiously steal from its citizens to avoid answering. Governments would function more like private enterprises, meaning those that were financially irresponsible would fail, making way for more prudent successors. Governments would be forced to satisfy citizens to survive because the money being spent would be real and scarce.

What does a government look like when it's bound by a moral economic system? What if politicians, kings, or even dictators lacked the ability to expand the money supply? When theft through inflation is no longer an option, *governments are forced to compete to serve the community.* This causes tax rates to become more market-driven, and therefore more affordable. At the same time, the government services improve since they are forced to compete for tax dollars. Even the most ruthless tyrant is limited by moral money.

Politics Become Cleaner

> *"A leader who is a great oppressor lacks understanding, but a person who hates unjust gain will prolong his days."* — Proverbs 28:16

Spending money that was created out of thin air and stolen from the community is an easy and effective way for politicians to promise free things. Those who want to win an election can promise anything they want because no explicit taxes have to be enacted to pay for it. As stated in Chapter 5, under our current monetary system, there are no real constraints or accountability.

It's easy to blame politicians for making promises that they can't keep, but they're not the only ones to blame. We have been complicit in this because we vote for politicians who promise the impossible. We have been trying to get something for nothing. The current monetary system has led us to believe that this is possible, and how we talk about politics is a symptom of its immoral and corrupt nature. Dirty politics are a result of the dirty monetary system.

On a Bitcoin standard, politicians would face real budget constraints and they wouldn't be able to make promises that they couldn't pay for. They would be held accountable for the *results* and not just the *intentions*. Consequently, the type of people going into politics would improve because those without the character to be accountable would be voted out.

Additionally, political jobs would require creativity to figure out the optimal tradeoffs of a real budget. In other words, politics would attract those who care for and want to see their communities improve. Further, political corruption would necessarily decline because the payoff from bribing political leaders would also be constrained by the budget. Bitcoin could simultaneously make politics less relevant in our lives and politicians more virtuous overall.

Disincentivizing War

> "Indeed, this is what the Lord says: 'Even the captives of the mighty man will be taken away, And the prey of a tyrant will be rescued; For I will contend with the one who contends with you, And I will save your sons.'" — Isaiah 49:25

Suppose a tyrant wants to start a war with a neighboring country. The dictator would need the support of the people, an army, and funding. The support of the people could be won with propaganda. An army could be acquired through conscription. The war, however, could not be funded without money, which governments can only raise through borrowing, taxation, or inflation. Wars are incredibly costly, and would require a tyrant to borrow, tax, or sell state-owned assets to engage in military action.

Under a bad monetary system, the tyrant could just print money and steal from the community. Instead of efficient and quick wars, the tyrant can afford to sustain conflicts. More people would die unnecessarily, and the community's resources would be drained for the war effort. Unbound by fiscal restraints, tyrants would impoverish their communities by funding war through inflation.

On a Bitcoin standard, a tyrant would face budget constraints and would have to practice good money management. The war would have to be fought intelligently and efficiently, and the tyrant would have to know when to stop to prevent bankruptcy—needing to carefully weigh all decisions and their tradeoffs during the war. All spending would necessitate careful consideration to efficiently deploy the precious resources the tyrant worked hard to accumulate.

Bitcoin creates other anti-war incentives. A government bound by scarce money will not want to kill off a vast percentage of the population through violent battles. This is because, without inflation, taxes become the main source of revenue, and killing off populations would reduce tax revenues.

War can also be extremely disruptive to economies, which are a source of tax revenues. A government operating a bad monetary system, on the other hand, doesn't have monetary constraints and would therefore be more inclined to be authoritarian. On a Bitcoin standard, human time is treasured, and citizens are valued.

Financial Access

> *"They only asked us to remember the poor—the very thing I also was eager to do."* — Galatians 2:10

There is a reason that 1.7 billion people don't have bank accounts. Setting up a bank account requires a visit to the bank, multiple forms of identification, and a source of funds. Maintaining a bank account can be even harder, with fees, account minimums, and overdraft penalties. Banks charge high fees for low-balance accounts because such accounts are not profitable. As a result, many poor households opt to keep whatever savings they have in cash, which is more liable to be stolen, either by physical theft or inflation.

For poor households, saving money is often more trouble than it's worth. Yet saving for the future is one of the only ways to get out of poverty. If we want to help the poor, we need to give them effective savings tools.

In our current system, saving money is doubly difficult. Not only are bank accounts costly and often inaccessible, but investments are complicated and expensive. There's a whole industry of financial professionals that get paid handsomely to navigate the complexities of various investments. The industry exists to outrun inflation, which naturally destroys savings.

Bitcoin can fix this. Bitcoin is a vehicle for long-term savings. Anyone with a phone or a computer can immediately set up a bitcoin wallet. No ID or bank is required, and the funds are secured digitally, making it difficult to steal. Because of its 21 million limit, Bitcoin holds its value better than any other money. Unlike gold, stocks, or real estate, Bitcoin can be bought in small amounts. Bitcoin gives financial access to those who need it most.

For those suffering under oppressive regimes, Bitcoin fixes an even more pernicious problem. Financial intermediaries often charge exorbitant rates and authoritarian governments steal the community's resources directly. Bitcoin's lack of a financial intermediary renders this kind of abuse and theft impossible. By cutting out middlemen, Bitcoin maximizes value and freedom for its holders.

Additionally, because Bitcoin is digital, transactions that were previously difficult become much easier. Consider sending dollars to a missionary in a closed country like Cuba. Financial intermediaries of all kinds take their cut and the process often takes weeks. Worse still, intermediaries can choose to censor the transaction. Sending Bitcoin is as easy as sending an email, and can be sent to anyone anywhere in the world in as little as 10 minutes without any third-party interference.

Improving Living Standards

> "The righteous person will flourish like the palm tree; he will grow like a cedar in Lebanon." — Psalm 92:12

As discussed in Chapter 6, the unfortunate effect of inflation is that goods and services degrade in quality over time. This is because of the phenomenon of sticky prices, where consumers refuse to pay more for the same goods, even if the money that they're paying with is worth less. Unlike a deflationary environment where goods and services constantly get better, there's a tendency under fiat money for goods and services to get worse.

As we move toward a Bitcoin standard, this changes. Goods and services priced in Bitcoin will become more affordable and improve significantly over time as technology develops. This is because people are more incentivized to save. Goods and services must appeal to customers more than saving money, which means they have to improve.

Craftsmanship and creativity get rewarded and items last longer and work better. Workers are incentivized to develop more skills and are judged based on their merit. In short, the quality of both goods and labor improves.

Fiat money's worth is constantly degrading due to inflation. Because the supply of Bitcoin is fixed, Bitcoin is a true measuring stick by which all other goods can be valued. On a Bitcoin standard, economic calculations become simpler, and in turn, allow entrepreneurs to make better decisions.

Less money, effort, and time is wasted on unworkable ideas, as those resources instead are redirected toward what the market demands. In other words, Bitcoin allows righteous living and civilization to flourish.

A Vote Against the Bloat

> *"The fallow ground of the poor would yield much food, but it is swept away through injustice."* — Proverbs 13:23

Much of our world is infected with endless amounts of bureaucracy: our schools, health care systems, and businesses all feed and grow on fiat money. Bureaucracy is an accumulation of bad decisions fueled by wasteful, debt-financed spending.

Long-term waste has created a multitude of meaningless, rent-seeking jobs leading to empty lives of going through the motions. Since these jobs don't provide any value, they are often given to friends and family, spreading the unjust practice of cronyism. Such meaningless work is detrimental to society and workers alike.

Bureaucratic waste is what causes healthcare to be too expensive, our governments to be ineffective, and our schools to be prisons for our kids. How much human life has been wasted by bureaucracy created from fiat money? Fortunately, Bitcoin gives us a solution.

Every Bitcoin purchased is a vote against bureaucratic bloat. Bitcoin fixes bureaucratic inefficiency because Bitcoin is scarce. More Bitcoin can't be printed to paper over mistakes. In this way, Bitcoin accounts for how money is spent. If it is spent in frivolous ways, there will not be a bailout. Bitcoin doesn't completely solve bureaucracy, but it does stop its fiat-induced cancerous growth.

On a Bitcoin standard, governments cannot print money to fund "make work" jobs like those comprising most bureaucracies. Bitcoin imposes accountability on governments, as wasteful spending cannot be obscured by inflation. Bureaucratic bloat will naturally shrink because Bitcoin adds fiscal constraints. In short, Bitcoin brings meaning back into the workplace.

This new standard of accountability brings a host of other benefits to the community. Because there is less waste, innovations in all aspects of society are able to thrive, attention is paid to the quality of goods, and the Earth's resources are better managed.

How does Bitcoin do this? How can Bitcoin have so many positive effects on society? It almost seems too good to be true. There is another deep reason that Bitcoin changes society for the better, and that is because Bitcoin causes people to properly value other people's time.

A New Perspective on Time

> *"Look carefully then how you walk, not as unwise but as wise, making the best use of the time, because the days are evil."*
> — Ephesians 5:15-16

Bitcoin helps its owners plan over the long term. Bitcoin doesn't degrade, which allows us to place more value on our time. Bitcoin causes us to value our time more because our labor can be stored in money that holds its value. As a result, we don't worry about money as much and are left free to pursue more meaningful work. Bitcoin reflects the scarce nature of time by being perfectly scarce.

When enough people change their perspective on work and time, profound changes occur in a community. We start valuing other people's time. We gain a deeper understanding of the past and make better plans for the future. We start saving for future generations instead of stealing from them. We start building up civilization instead of tearing it down.

Our current mentality is a sick and twisted one. If we don't value other people's time, we are not loving them. The core evil pervading our wasteful bureaucratic systems is that they have stolen billions of hours of human time. We can act against this evil by using money that better reflects the value of human time. Bitcoin helps us to love our neighbor and helps us lead purposeful lives.

Strong Families

> "God blessed them; and God said to them, 'Be fruitful and multiply, and fill the earth, and subdue it; and rule over the fish of the sea and over the birds of the sky and over every living thing that moves on the earth.'" — Genesis 1:28

As discussed in Chapter 6, our current monetary system incentivizes consumption and high time preference behavior. This is because money expands quickly enough that saving it is not worthwhile, and the consequence is an increase in consumption. The emphasis on consumption has negative consequences upon how we view people.

Birth rates are going down in every first-world nation, and one of the biggest reasons is because children are seen as a bad tradeoff. Children are seen as expensive, time consuming, and difficult to manage. The average person has a high-time preference, which causes them to focus on immediate comforts. Children are seen as liabilities, not blessings. These concerns have been true for all of human history, yet in an era when we have the most material comforts, people are having fewer children than ever.

The reason is because our society views people primarily as consumers or as problems to be solved rather than as problem solvers. This is why we may view children as liabilities who consume our wealth, rather than as assets and blessings.

On a Bitcoin standard, this changes. Instead of thinking about the short-term pain of child rearing, Bitcoin frees people to have a more expansive view of time. This enables the long-term blessing of children to be more evident. A longer time horizon helps us to see children as essential contributors to the health and sustainability of the community and not as short-term financial liabilities.

This will result in more stable marriages and more children. This will also remove the fear and urgency that motivates many abortions. Parents who live with a low time preference are more likely to produce children who make low time preference decisions. Children who understand that work produces abundance are far more likely to grow into productive adults and less likely to be reliant on the government. Children such as these are indeed blessings, not liabilities.

Bitcoin also has the potential to help alleviate some of the financial stress that can fracture families. Since Bitcoin incentivizes saving, people will be better prepared to handle costs associated with later stages of life. Our elderly will be less likely to be seen as burdens if we can care for them in a proper and affordable manner. Healthier families will, in turn, produce healthier communities.

A Church Economic Reformation

> *"Do not conform to the pattern of this world, but be transformed by the renewing of your mind. Then you will be able to test and approve what God's will is—his good, pleasing and perfect will."*
> — Romans 12:2

The mission of the Church is to deliver hope to a broken world. We cannot do that while entrenched in our own sin. However, reforming the Church is politically and spiritually difficult. Throughout history the Church has faced many problems, from the New Testament debate about circumcision to the Medieval practice of selling Indulgences.

As the scripture in Romans says, we are not supposed to conform to this world but be transformed. This transformation only happens once we are confronted with the truth and accept its ramifications.

With the understanding of how fiat money has led to corruption and erosion in the Church, we can finally start to repair the damage that has been done. As discussed in Chapter 7, churches have succumbed to the temptation of easy money and are now burdened by massive debt because of it. This has caused churches to focus on worldly matters instead of pursuing God.

The question is, how do we move forward from here?

The first step to any reform is confession. As a Church, we must confess to our obsession with money and ask God for forgiveness. Recognizing that we've gone astray and have prioritized financial prosperity instead of holiness is no easy task, especially because most churches do not believe they are prioritizing financial prosperity.

It's time for the Church to strongly consider the effects of the fiat monetary system they operate under and move toward actively separating themselves from it. Consider this a call for a new economic reformation in the Church. The Church is made up of people. Therefore, an economic reformation of the Church requires the economic reformation of the congregants. Ministries to help people get out of financial ruts, and provide a better understanding of fiat money's corrupting effects are good first steps. Helping the money-obsessed recover from their addiction is another.

Bitcoin can help with this. Congregants can learn to let go of short-term pleasures and practice the virtue of prudence. Instead of a congregation held down by debt and miserable rent-seeking jobs, what would a congregation full of debt-free followers of Christ be able to do? A church full of people free from money worship and solely devoted to God would be a powerful force for good.

Restoring Justice

> *"You shall not distort justice, you shall not show partiality; and you shall not accept a bribe, because a bribe blinds the eyes of the wise and distorts the words of the righteous."* — Deuteronomy 16:19

We have laid out the many ways in which the ills of our current monetary system could be fixed with Bitcoin. Money is a medium through which we express our values and preferences. Therefore, Bitcoin's many benefits extend beyond the monetary realm and into the moral and spiritual realms.

Because money is so pervasive, bad money corrupts all aspects of life. The most important of these is our character and specifically how we treat others. Bad money has tempted everyone to steal from the community instead of bearing God's image by working to create something with our hands. Theft at the highest levels changes the rules of money itself, tilting the playing field toward those in power, and dispossessing the rest.

So much of the societal strife that plagues the world today has been directly caused by our corrupt monetary system. As explained in Chapters 3 and 4, the rich are able to get richer through government grift and access to cheap debt. The poor, on the other hand, are kept poor with high rates of interest and a lack of sound savings technologies. Much of the social unrest we see today is because of this obvious injustice.

A significant failing of the fiat monetary system is that its rules are unsound. How many US dollars are in circulation? Who gets to decide? On what criteria are they deciding? Who is profiting from their production? Not only are these rules unclear, but they are subject to change. Stable rules lead to stable communities, and when rules are breakable, relationships break down. The fixed rules of Bitcoin engender justice, fairness, and peace.

Bitcoin is an incorruptible money, one whose rules cannot be changed without the entire community's consent. The self-sovereignty of each individual is respected, and theft is made very difficult. Bitcoin redeems much of what has been corrupted by fiat money, and in a sense, Bitcoin is the fulfillment of what money is supposed to be.

Under a Bitcoin system, rent-seeking opportunities will be reduced, and people will earn money in proportion to the value they provide the community. Instead of money being a weapon wielded by the powerful, money will be an impartial judge getting distributed to those who fulfill the community's needs. In other words, a Bitcoin standard would restore monetary justice to the world.

What Bitcoin Doesn't Fix

> *"I am the Lord your God, who brought you out of the land of Egypt, out of the house of slavery."* — Exodus 20:2

Bitcoin fixes many of the corruptions of our current monetary system. Bitcoin, however, is not a panacea.

Assuming that Bitcoin continues on its path, the temptation will be to love it, rejoice in it, trust it supremely, and to judge all those that didn't get on board early enough. This temptation toward pride is one that we must fight with everything we have. Many have fallen into this trap with Bitcoin. It's a better, more moral money, but due to its rapid monetization, it's been a way for many to "get rich quick."

The gratification of not only gaining wealth fast, but also being correct about a novel tech holds the danger of breeding greed and egoism. The goal is to create a world more aligned with God to the benefit of others, not to seek meaning in material wealth. If monetary gain becomes our goal and focus, we have already lost.

What do you have that you did not receive? Were you drawn to Bitcoin while your friends and family were uninterested? Were you just lucky? It doesn't matter. Whatever wealth we get from Bitcoin is only useful to God if we use it to love God and our neighbors.

Good money is a gift that can help us be better, but it is not an end in and of itself. Bitcoin was made by human hands, and the temptation has always been to worship the work of our own hands. We must fight this temptation and instead focus on living lives in humble love and service to others.

Why Not Return to Gold?

> *"Like a dog that returns to its vomit,*
> *So is a fool who repeats his foolishness."*
> — Proverbs 26:11

Many books written about sound money promote the hope that governments would bring back the gold standard. Generally, the call to action at the end of these books is to educate and inform others about what sound money is. Their hope is that there would eventually be enough people who agree on the importance of bringing back the gold standard to take political action.

The unfortunate reality is that the world has moved past gold. The physical nature of gold makes it impractical to use as money. In our day and age, the world is increasingly reliant on digital transactions. The alternative to physical trading of gold is gold-backed money. This has been tried many times throughout history and it has morphed each time into fiat money. Going back to a gold standard is rife with all manner of temptations and it inevitably leads to centralized control over gold reserves.

Even if countries returned to a gold standard, there would always be the possibility of a return to fiat money because of a financial intermediary that could be coerced. In other words, gold has failed us multiple times in the past and going back to gold is not a practical solution.

Gradually, Then Suddenly

> *"But be on your guard, so that your hearts will not be weighed down with dissipation and drunkenness and the worries of life, and that this day will not come on you suddenly, like a trap;"* — Luke 21:34

Those in political power are disincentivized to go back to a gold standard. Too many powerful people, many of whom are in government, benefit too much from the current monetary system. Our political and banking classes are heavily invested in the benefits that fiat money grants them. These interests wield a huge amount of power, so it would be naïve to think that they would revert to a monetary system that would limit that power. For these two reasons, the hope of going back to gold is naive.

Unlike gold, Bitcoin can be adopted gradually. Instead of requiring a political majority, individuals can choose to adopt it without overhauling the existing system. There's also no trust involved. People won't need to go from trusting one system to another. Bitcoin holders can be their own bank. There is no single point of control, there are less worries about confiscation, and there is more power in the hands of individuals. Further, because Bitcoin is digital, it's much easier to secure and transfer than a physical commodity. This lowers the barriers to adoption for the entire community.

The potential for a gradual adoption of Bitcoin is a major strength and gives us a path toward sound money that isn't dependent on political wrangling. Everyone has the choice to adopt Bitcoin when it is best for them, and in a way that best suits their needs. As Bitcoin's benefits are realized by the community, individuals will be more inclined to adopt it. In other words, Bitcoin can win through competition on the free market instead of having to be imposed on the community like fiat money. Bitcoin exists independent of the political system.

Bitcoin Fixes Us

> "Yet God has made everything beautiful for its own time. He has planted eternity in the human heart, but even so, people cannot see the whole scope of God's work from beginning to end. So I concluded there is nothing better than to be happy and enjoy ourselves as long as we can. And people should eat and drink and enjoy the fruits of their labor, for these are gifts from God." — Ecclesiastes 3:11

Existing in a temporal body while being consciously aware of eternity is a paradoxical condition of the human experience. We are often hung up on the past, anxious about the future, and struggle to remain in the present moment. Accepting the simple wisdom of Ecclesiastes does not come naturally. We don't easily recognize the gifts God offers us every day because we are too distracted by worldly forces that constantly compete for our attention and energy.

God continues to be at work in the world, even today. This hasn't always been a radical statement for Christians. Identifying the ways God continues to provide practical gifts and hopeful solutions for our biggest problems is what it means to testify. It's no wonder thanking God for Bitcoin can seem petty or unserious. However, we must reckon with the multitude of ways that Bitcoin offers hope for humanity and attribute this gift to a loving and benevolent God.

Bitcoin is an invitation to slow down long enough to see God's hands at work amid the chaos. The emergence of a practical alternative to the modern-day Mammon is an invitation to step off the fiat treadmill and become more aware of every good and perfect gift we've received.

For instance, it's impossible to delight in the unique qualities of a child, if we are constantly lamenting how fast they grow up and fretting about various aspects of their future as adults. The saying that "kids growing up too fast" is itself an indication of a hurried lifestyle. That hurried lifestyle is the result of underlying economic fears we carry due to the corruption of our money. An appropriate relationship with time helps us embrace each stage of a child's development as being beautiful in its own right.

The issues we've identified throughout this book can feel daunting… because they are. We can't sugarcoat or neglect our obligation to stand against the abysmal state of affairs we face. The good news is that Bitcoin offers us hope that we can overcome these existential challenges.

This is not an untested theory. Many communities of Bitcoiners are already living into the promise of a new world, rooted in sound money, and eschewing the bondage of fiat. The book that you are holding is a perfect example of how Bitcoin brings people together for a common purpose and allows us to transcend the divisive categories offered by the old world.

Conclusion

Our current monetary system is stagnant, unsecure, monopolistic, entrenched, intermediated, censorable, and immoral. Its current design allows significant theft and causes problems in the personal, political, and spiritual realms. We're caught in the worship of money, in a sort of monetary Stockholm Syndrome because of its enslaving nature. Our corrupt monetary system has even affected churches, many of which are more financially irresponsible than they'd like to admit.

Bitcoin is innovative, secure, competitive, disruptive, highly accessible, uncensorable, and moral. Bitcoin removes stealth theft through inflation, runaway government spending, and misaligned political incentives. Bitcoin repairs our dysfunctional relationship with money, brings more meaning to our time and work, incentivizes prudence, and frees us from debt enslavement. Bitcoin repairs our communities, provides financial access to the poor, aligns community incentives, and allows us to save and plan for the future. Bitcoin is nothing less than the redemption of our corrupt monetary system.

Given all of Bitcoin's benefits, it is no surprise adoption is growing. However, the full redemption of money requires the community's adoption. Only when Bitcoin becomes the de facto currency of a majority of the community will it become the standard. Then and only then will the full benefits for the community be realized. As a source of indisputable monetary truth in the world, Bitcoin can be the foundation for a more honest community.

That said, we don't have to wait for the community to adopt Bitcoin to receive its benefits. We can experience the change in perspective that comes from being free of the shackles of our corrupt monetary system one person at a time. Bitcoin gives us a way to renounce the worship of money. We can then understand and experience money as the gift from God that it truly is.

Money is a means to trade, and trade is a means for creating useful things for the community's benefit. Money, in other words, is a necessary ingredient for the fullest expression of who God created us to be. Bad money hinders us from our purpose and draws us toward the worship of created things rather than the Creator. Good money helps us fulfill our purpose and brings us closer to God.

Until Bitcoin, good money was not something we could freely choose. We now have a tool to combat our obsession with money and put money in its proper place. For this, we should express our gratitude to God.

You were asked at the start of this book what you thought of when you heard the word "money." The response is typically some mix of fear, anxiety, and greed. It doesn't have to be this way. Money is a gift, and if we realize God's intention for it, we will gain a new appreciation and fresh perspective on our purpose. As this attitude is internalized, our thoughts on money will become "Thank God for Bitcoin."

Afterword

IN THE FIVE YEARS since the publication of Thank God for Bitcoin, its global impact has far exceeded our expectations. The book has opened the hearts and minds of readers, renewing the faith journey for some, and revealing the power of Bitcoin for others. The underlying message has resonated in profound ways: both Christians and non-Christians worldwide have used the book to initiate conversations about the monetary system with church elders, politicians, missionaries and business leaders.

The book has been translated into seven languages—Spanish, French, Portuguese, Korean, Dutch, Finnish, and Estonian—with ongoing requests for more. This response catalyzed the formation of TGFB Media, led by co-author JM Bush, teaching Christians about the morality of sound money through the 'Thank God for Bitcoin,' and 'Thank God for Nostr' podcasts, an annual conference, and other Christ-centered events uniting Christians and Bitcoiners. These efforts have fostered a global Christian Bitcoin community, enabling cross-cultural church partnerships and missionary strategies that deliver resources swiftly and securely.

We have spoken with multiple missionary organizations that utilize Bitcoin to fund ministries in countries isolated from the SWIFT system due to war or sanctions. Churches and other nonprofits have taken a small Bitcoin position with their reserves and have seen those funds significantly outperform the rest of their portfolios, granting them greater funding flexibility at a time when many other organizations are struggling to combat inflation. A school in Paraguay initiated mining Bitcoin as a side project to offset its costs and ultimately expanded the operation due to its profitability. There are thousands of individuals and families saving in Bitcoin who have been more generous with their time and wealth. Many Christian missions from combating sex slavery in Uganda to church plants in Cuba have benefited from such giving. There are hundreds more of these stories and many more that can't be told because of the sensitive nature of the work involved.

Further, there are an increasing number of Christian organizations working to leverage Bitcoin for kingdom impact. Brilliance Labs and the Magnalia Foundation are both non-profit organizations that are working to help orange-pill the missions world and stateside church world, respectively. The Bitcoin Beach project, founded by Mike Peterson and his best friend, a pastor named Pete Desoto, have done groundbreaking work in the beachfront village of El Zonte in El Salvador. Their world has inspired similar works in Peru, Uruguay, in a variety of countries in Africa, and many more. And as of this second printing, TGFB Media will be becoming a non-profit to continue to help the global Church understand and use Bitcoin for the glory of God and the good of people everywhere.

But perhaps the biggest surprise has been the number of Bitcoiners who have read this book and have cited it as a motivation for attending church. At nearly every conference, we meet Bitcoiners who have since started seeking Christ, with many getting baptized into the faith. There seems to be something about learning the truth about money that leads people into exploring greater spiritual truths. In response, TGFB published its first dedicated resource designed to provide food for thought for faith-curious Bitcoiners, a book called *The Gospel According To Bitcoin*.

Since the book's release, Bitcoin itself has achieved unprecedented adoption. As of September 2025, it holds a market capitalization of over $2 trillion. It is legal in over 130 countries, with seven government treasuries collectively holding more than 500,000 BTC (valued at billions). Millions more people now own Bitcoin in lieu of fiat currency with more options than ever all over the globe to buy and sell with it.

Scripture addresses money over 2,000 times, with Jesus using financial metaphors to illuminate spiritual truths. Yet, the church has overlooked the immorality of the current monetary system. This rerelease includes subtle updates at the edges, but the main content of the book remains the same: God calls for 'just weights and measures' (Leviticus 19:35-36; Proverbs 11:1), which directly condemns monetary debasement and the violation of this principle has severe consequences at all different levels. Bitcoin's encoded fixed supply of

AFTERWORD

21 million coins and decentralization better aligns with God's design, making for a more moral money.

We are deeply grateful to the many supporters within both the Christian and Bitcoin communities. Please join us at tgfb.com and on telegram at https://t.me/thankgodforbitcoin.

ROBERT BREEDLOVE, J.M. BUSH, GABE HIGGINS, GEORGE MEKHAIL, LYLE PRATT, JIMMY SONG, JULIA TOURIANSKI, AND DEREK WALTCHACK

Acknowledgements

THIS BOOK is the result of a Bible study that we formed during the lockdowns of 2020. In addition to biblical reading, we studied several books on the topic of monetary ethics. Jörg Guido Hülsmann's *Ethics of Money Production* and Gary North's *Honest Money* inspired us, and helped us reason through many of the arguments in *Thank God For Bitcoin*.

We would like to thank the following people for providing early reviews of the manuscript: Rosa Shores, Robert William Allen, Eryka Gemma, Parker White, Britt Neel, Julie Neel, Jason Malinak, Caleb Lind, Marc Mckirahan, Matthew Hanzelka, Brian Harrington, Guilherme Bandeira, Nate Sharp, Dan Rempel, Taylor Fletcher, Arthur Amendt, John Balauat, Linda Goetze, Valentina Topolskaia, and Adam Slusher.

We would like to thank the editors that we hired from UpWork, Sarah Lamb, Allison Hestor and Bonita Jewel, and Rob Hewitt, who typeset and designed the cover for the second edition. We also owe Tyler Torti a huge debt of gratitude for volunteering to re-record the audiobook for us for free. The end product is much better for it.

We're very thankful to our spouses and children who granted us the time needed for the completion of this work: Julie Song, Jimmy's kids (T, L, M, T, L and M), Sara Bush, J.M.'s kids (J, E, A, A, and E), Gabe's kids (M, T, A, T, L, E and A), Danielle Mekhail, Kingston Mekhail, Saxyn Mekhail, Rushton Waltchack, Rollins Waltchack, Anne Rainey Waltchack, Henry Waltchack, Mei Sims Waltchack, Colley Waltchack, Mimi Waltchack, Janet Pamplin, Robert's kid (P), Julia Tourianski's husband and kids, and Lyle's family: Aurelia and Cosette. Finally, we are thankful to God, for everything.

About the Authors

ROBERT BREEDLOVE is a Bitcoin-focused entrepreneur, writer, podcaster, and philosopher. Robert considers himself a Freedom Maximalist and believes he has found his life's work in the Bitcoin space as a contributor to the separation of money and state. He grew up in southern Baptist churches and now considers himself a non-denominational disciple of Christ. Find Robert on X (@Breedlove22) and Instagram (@Breedlove_22) where he posts about Bitcoin, economics, and philosophy. A current list of Robert's work can be found at: breedlove.io

J.M. BUSH was a churchplanting missionary in Montevideo, Uruguay and is now the executive director of TGFB Media (tgfb.com), which helps Christians understand and use Bitcoin for the glory of God and the good of people everywhere. He is a husband, father of five, and has co-authored two other books: 'The Gospel According To Bitcoin' and 'The Orange Umbrella.' He blogs at economicsofglory.substack.com. You can follow him on X @jordanbush.

GABE HIGGINS is a husband, father, entrepreneur, musician, and technologist. He discovered Bitcoin in 2012 right after learning about the role of central banking in monetary policy from former Congressman Ron Paul. Gabe's interest in technology, economics and being philosophically libertarian precipitated his interest in being an early adopter and advocate for Bitcoin. He founded *Tampa Bay Bitcoin* in 2014, the world's longest running Bitcoin meetup, and co-founded *BlockSpaces*, focused on building Bitcoin software solutions. Gabe serves on the board of *Save The Kids Foundation* and advisor to *Bitcoin Bay Foundation* and on the worship team at his church. You can follow him on X @GabeBHiggins.

GEORGE MEKHAIL is the Managing Director of Bitcoin for Corporations at BTC Inc., author of *I Am Not Your Bruh*, and co-author of *Thank God for Bitcoin*. A passionate advocate for Bitcoin since 2017, George blends his experience in marketing, financial innovation, and community development to guide companies in thoughtfully integrating Bitcoin into their strategic operations, while also advocating for strong family dynamics at home.

LYLE PRATT is an investor, programmer, entrepreneur, and the Founder & CEO of Vida.io, an enterprise-grade AI voice company. Before Vida, he founded a number of companies including BetterVoice, which was later acquired by Inteliquent (NASDAQ: IQNT). Lyle holds an MBA in Finance, an MS in Engineering and Technology Management, and a BS in Business Economics from Louisiana Tech University. He is also a LP and Advisor at Trammell Venture Partners. Outside of work, he enjoys Bitcoin, boating, brazilian jiu-jitsu, liberty, tech, and family life. Find him on X at @lylepratt.

JIMMY SONG is a Bitcoin programmer, educator and entrepreneur. He was born in Seoul, South Korea, where his devout maternal grandmother exposed him to the Gospel. He immigrated to the US as an eight-year-old when his family started attending a Korean Presbyterian church. He's attended a wide variety of churches from Vineyard and Hillsong to Presbyterian and Southern Baptist, and many in between. He currently attends Tarrytown Christian Church which started meeting in someone's backyard during the pandemic. He's been told he bears a striking resemblance to Francis Chan. He's written four other books, including Programming Bitcoin, The Little Bitcoin Book, Bitcoin and the American Dream and Fiat Ruins Everything. He can be found on X @jimmysong and his newsletter at jimmysong.substack.com.

JULIA TOURIANSKI was one of the first "Bitcoin evangelists," and is the author of "The Declaration of Bitcoin's Independence." In her past life she ran the YouTube channel "Brave The World" where she talked Guns, God, Government, and everything in-between. She is currently retired, raising her 4 children and 3 geese.

ABOUT THE AUTHORS

DEREK WALTCHACK is an entrepreneur, investor, and lifelong builder who discovered Bitcoin in 2015 and has been captivated ever since. He is the co-founder of Shannon Waltchack, a Birmingham-based commercial real estate investment firm known for transforming small neighborhood shopping centers into long-lasting community assets. Derek also hosts the *Brokerlord Podcast*, where he helps real estate brokers think like owners and build wealth. A graduate from Samford University he is an active member of Covenant Presbyterian Church (PCA), where he met his wife, Rushton. Together they are raising six children—an energetic crew that keeps them grounded, joyful, and always looking toward the future. You can follow him on X @dwaltchack.

Resources

Christian Bitcoin Books

— *The Gospel According to Bitcoin* by Dan Sherman and JM Bush
— *The Bible and Bitcoin* by Alin Armstrong

Bitcoin History

— *The Genesis Book* by Aaron von Wirdum
— *The Blocksize War* by Jonathan Bier
— *The Big Print* by Larry Lepard

Bitcoin Economics

— *The Bitcoin Standard* by Saifedean Ammous
— *The Bullish Case for Bitcoin* by Vijay Boyapati, available at https://medium.com/@vijayboyapati/the-bullish-case-for-bitcoin-6ecc8bdecc1
— *Gradually, Then Suddenly* by Parker Lewis
— *Broken Money* by Lyn Alden

Bitcoin Technical Details (Easy)

- *The Little Bitcoin Book* by The Bitcoin Collective
- *Bitcoin Clarity* by Kiara Bickers
- *Inventing Bitcoin* by Yan Pritzker

Bitcoin Technical Details (Hard)

- *Bitcoin: A Peer-to-Peer Electronic Cash System* by Satoshi Nakamoto, available at https://nakamotoinstitute.org/bitcoin/
- *Grokking Bitcoin* by Kalle Rosenbaum
- *Programming Bitcoin* by Jimmy Song
- *Bitcoin Miner's Almanac* by Robert Warren

Bitcoin Kids Books

- *The Orange Umbrella* by JM Bush and JD Ryan
- *Bitcoin Money* by Michael Caras
- *A Treasure To Hodl* by Lindey Magee

Websites

- https://tgfb.com
- Resource for all things Bitcoin-related at https://lopp.net/bitcoin
- Further Bitcoin reading and resources: https://bitcoin-resources.com

Made in the USA
Coppell, TX
21 February 2026

72484632R00085